The Making of

THE INDEPENDENT

THE MAKING OF

INDEPENDENT

Michael Crozier

Gordon Fraser · London

First published 1988 by
Gordon Fraser Gallery Ltd, London and Bedford
Copyright © Michael Crozier 1988

BRITISH LIBRARY CATALOGUING IN PUBLICATION DATA

Crozier, Michael
The Making of 'The Independent'.
1. Newspapers with London imprints.
Independent, The
I. Title
072′.1

ISBN 0 86092 107 7

The publishers would like to thank the proprietors of *The
Independent* for their co-operation and for permission to
reproduce copyright material in this book.

Text set and printed by The Alden Press, Oxford
Bound by Hunter and Foulis Ltd, Edinburgh
Designed by Sarah Menon

Contents

Foreword

I had always hoped that *Today* would be the first of a new breed of national newspapers which would create a wider base of ownership than was currently available in Britain and a greater choice of titles for the reading public. But that was not to be.

Because of the union threat to 'strangle *Today* at birth', we had no alternative but to build our own presses, set up our own distribution networks and put ourselves outside the sphere of militant union influence. This proved to be our biggest problem as we struggled to overcome the logistics of the launch and never had time to concentrate on the content of the paper and its market.

In the end the print unions were an irrelevance. Already weakened by the dispute between the Warrington Messenger and the NGA, they were finally broken at the barbed wire gate of Wapping.

With this background, *Today*'s launch came and went, as did its public support and its money. The paper soon came under Lonrho's ownership. The dream of a new national newspaper industry, based on fresh ideas, on new technology and free from restrictive practices which brought their own censorship, had foundered.

The soon-to-be-launched *Independent* became the standard bearer of the new order.

Unlike *Today*, with its hype and public support, *The Independent* was said to have no chance in an already overcrowded and limited market. It had no colour, no real advantage other than the fresh spirit of its journalists, its ideals and an innovative and quietly determined leader in Andreas Whittam Smith.

I had met Andreas when he first came up with the idea of a new quality newspaper based on independent values. We had discussed the future of the industry and both felt that new technology and broken union practices could result in a new breed of newspapers being created.

As I struggled on with *Today*, Andreas and his team put together a firm creative and financial base from which to launch *The Independent*.

It has often been said that they learnt from our mistakes. I don't think that was entirely true for we spoke little during those days. The great advantage that they had was in not worrying about the printing and distribution logistics. It was a luxury that they fully exploited. It gave them the time to concentrate on their product and their market. The launch of *The Independent* showed that they had used that time well.

Although criticised for being bland, the new paper soon built up a steady and loyal readership. What the critics had not taken into account was that any new product takes time to establish itself. *The Independent* did it sooner than most.

I have heard that I played a small part in the creation of *The Independent*. I wish that were true.

The real truth is that *The Independent* was the result of one man's belief and passion, and in this he was ably supported by financiers, colleagues and journalists who worked with him to make the dream a reality.

The Independent is the bedrock for a new newspaper industry. I hope other publishers, spurred on by its success, will use the new low costs within the industry to launch their own dreams.

And, in time, that will bring about a truly free press with a wider base of ownership and a multiplicity of titles satisfying varying sectors of the community. If that happens, then *The Independent* will be seen not just as a good newspaper, but as the first of a new generation.

Eddie Shah,
Chairman of The Messenger Newspaper Group Ltd.

Preface

The story of *The Independent* has aroused interest around the world. From the dream in the mind of an ambitious financial journalist to the raising of £18 million of launch capital to the investment in the most up-to-date technology, it is an intriguing story. I have tried to distance myself as far as possible and act as a reporter with access to good, inside information and not as a semi-official historian – the official history will come later, from the pen, typewriter or, most likely, computer of another author.

If I have allowed too much journalistic jargon slip through, the glossary at the back of the book should solve the mystery.

My thanks go to all the journalists of *The Independent*, whether they contributed to this book consciously or not; to my wife, Lee, for her help and support; Sarah Heneghan, who provided valuable research; Nick May for his artwork; James Fergusson for his critical eye; Tom Attwood and Bruce Fireman for patiently explaining how the finance was raised; lastly, and importantly, to Peter Knight, my agent, and Peter Guy, my publisher, for commissioning such an enjoyable project.

M.C.
London, 1988.

The eagle has landed: Celebrations at the launch night party with Andreas
Whittam Smith, *centre*; behind him is Matthew Symonds, Deputy Editor.

1: The Dream

And I dream of the days when work was scrappy,
And rare in our pockets the mark of the mint,
And we were angry and poor and happy,
And proud of seeing our names in print.

G.K. Chesterton (1874–1936)

It is fitting for this story that Daniel Defoe, the first of the great popular journalists, was buried in Bunhill Fields, in City Road, London next to the building where *The Independent* was going to be launched 255 years later.

Many famous Nonconformists and writers are buried there, including Blake and John Bunyan. Opposite is the Wesley Chapel – spiritual home and secular dwelling of John Wesley, founder of Methodism and sermoniser extraordinary. John Milton, who lived in nearby Bunhill Row for a time, wrote *Paradise Regained* there. The area is redolent with the skill and inspiration of these great writers. Their spirit hangs unseen over the modern-day scribes daily producing thousands of words read all over Britain.

Fate, will and a keen sense of enterprise brought the latterday nonconformists, who founded the newspaper, to such an apposite location in the early part of 1986. It was a literary home from home and was the result of months of determined effort and acute business acumen.

Early in 1985, Andreas Whittam Smith was comfortably installed in the City Editor's chair at *The Daily Telegraph*. He had been there for seven years, part of a distinguished career spanning 23 years in financial journalism, a career which had begun in a bizarre fashion.

He was born on 13 June 1937. His father, Canon J.E.Smith, was a vicar in Macclesfield. When he was three he moved to Birkenhead where his father took over a dockland parish. After attending Birkenhead School where his teachers thought he would not qualify for Oxbridge, he exhibited early signs of independence and self-determination by applying on his own to Keble College, Oxford.

After National Service during which he was told that he was 'unfit to lead men' he took his place at Oxford to read PPE – politics, philosophy and economics. His stay ended with a shock – he was awarded a Third Class degree which he never took. On leaving Oxford he was determined to do something in the City, a world away from the docks at Birkenhead.

In 1960 he was offered a job by N.M.Rothschild, the famous merchant bankers in the City of London, as a clerk checking bills of lading for the shipment of human hair from China. His pay was abysmal. Some time later he was introduced by chance to the editor of the *Glasgow Herald* who reckoned that since AWS worked for Rothschild he must know a lot about the City. AWS did not, but he soon learnt, after he boldly accepted a job on the newspaper writing a weekly column. After some persuasion, the *Financial Times* newspaper library provided him with all the necessary files for his articles and his career in City journalism had begun.

In 1962, he took a job on the *Stock Exchange Gazette*, later to become the *Investors Chronicle*. After this further period of training in the ways and wiles of the City, he moved in 1963 to the *Financial Times* and then in 1964 to *The Times*. In 1966, at the age of 29, he landed the job as Deputy City Editor of *The Daily Telegraph*. He was, and is still, very ambitious and in 1969 became City Editor of *The Guardian* setting up the City pages in a matter of weeks.

A year later his restless feet took him to the *Investors Chronicle* which he was to edit for seven years. In 1977 he returned to *The Daily Telegraph* as City Editor. The pattern was set. He had built up an impressive network of friends in the City and, more importantly, knew how it worked.

Early in March 1985, two days after Eddie Shah, newspaper owner and leading advocate of new technology, had announced that he intended to start a new national colour daily to be published seven days a week, AWS was rung up by a journalist from *Business Week* magazine and asked whether he thought it would work.

He said no, but as soon as he put the telephone down, he realised that he was wrong. The idea of starting his own newspaper had been planted in his mind. AWS prides himself on his ability to recognise turning points in business and politics, and to make forecasts. He felt then that Shah was the turning point and that the newspaper industry would never be the same again. The parlous economic state of *The Telegraph* at the time was crucial to his future motivation.

'Throughout the first part of 1985 it was evident that *The Daily Telegraph* was in an extremely bad way, the circulation was falling off every month. There was an air of crisis and panic,' explained AWS. But at the same time that he began to believe in the viability of Shah's project, he also began to devise a way of saving *The Telegraph*, to stop it from falling into other hands.

This is a forceful example of AWS's philosophy: 'I've always had a twin-track mind. I like to advance in two directions at the same time.' If one course of action did not succeed he could fall back on the other.

He rang Eddie Shah the day after the telephone call from *Business Week* and asked to meet him although he was not thinking of working for the new paper. Already his ideas about his own newspaper were strengthening. He decided that there was no need to set up new printing plants because the spare capacity of existing plants around the country could be used. Plants where evening newspapers are printed lie dormant from the early afternoon until the following morning – an ideal situation for the production of a morning newspaper. Before having a breakfast meeting with Shah he rang Graeme Walsh at Morgan Grenfell, the merchant bankers, on 22 March and asked him whether his very early plans for a newspaper could be financed. AWS's guesstimate on costings was then £10 or £11 million. The answer was 'yes, subject to 1,000 conditions'.

His anger towards reactionary and intransigent newspaper management was growing ever stronger at this time. Although he liked Lord Hartwell, proprietor of *The Daily Telegraph*, he felt deep resentment at having to work under the whims of an owner who very possibly did not understand the economics of modern newspapers and who seemed embarked on a course of action which would culminate in his beloved newspaper being sold off cheaply to an entrepreneur. At that stage too, he believed he had a 50 per cent chance of succeeding William Deedes, then 71, as Editor of *The Daily Telegraph*.

On 25 March he wrote a memo to himself, saying that his new paper would be a national broadsheet aimed at a readership taken from the top end of the *Daily Mail* and from *The Daily Telegraph* and *The Times*. It would have wide appeal to a younger readership and would be strongly libertarian. There would be an edition at midnight. The average age of the staff would be about 35 with no one over 50. It would be produced through new technology with journalists typing their stories directly into a computer and with full-page on-screen layout. There was to be no distinction between writers and sub-editors at this stage. He wanted all employees to have shares in the business and journalists would have control over the entire operation. He had no firm ideas then about what the circulation should or would be.

He had a certain number of specific questions to put to Eddie Shah which would further catalyse his ideas. He wanted to know what the position of the unions would be in Shah's new enterprise and how a system of franchise distribution would actually work. What would the management structure be? Would the new distribution system be available to others?

The editorial formula was also beginning to consolidate. In another memo he wrote to himself a few days later, he decided that the newspaper would reflect the free market economy with an emphasis on news rather than publishing. There would be weekly coverage of science, technology and education. On 31 March he wrote prophetically: 'I am now inclined to think that proclaiming an independent standpoint is actually making a definite position on the political spectrum.'

On launch strategy and a timetable, he wrote: 'The key problem is the conservatism of the daily newspaper industry. How could one change the habits of a lifetime?' He felt that the money should be raised by September 1985 and that the paper would be set up in April 1986 and launched in October 1986.

The next step was to see if advertisers would be interested in his new project. He had already contacted Maurice Saatchi of Saatchi and Saatchi, the world's biggest advertising agency, who in turn put him in touch with John Perriss, then head of Saatchi's media buying department. Saatchi said that if AWS could convince Perriss, 'the most powerful media buyer in Britain', of the viability of his project then he was on his way. Perriss was told by Saatchi to be as doom-laden as possible; to tell AWS that it was fantastic-ally difficult to set up a newspaper, that the advertising account directors were incredibly conservative people, and probably would not support such a new venture. However AWS was able to convince Perriss of the strength of the project and Saatchi agreed to help with initial market research and give him access to their computer data on readership and advertising statistics.

At about the same time as he was writing himself memos about what type of newspaper it should be, AWS decided he needed one or more partners for his fledgling venture. He knew Matthew Symonds, then 31, who had joined *The Daily Telegraph* in November 1981 and succeeded Jock Bruce Gardyne as economic leader writer; he had also been producing a fortnightly economic column for the City pages. AWS thought very highly of Symonds' abilities and considered him to be one of the brightest talents to join the newspaper for a long time. For several months they had collaborated on articulating the economic and business policies of the newspaper and, after a degree of management inertia, had produced a major survey on unemployment in Britain which was later turned into a pamphlet. In doing so they had to learn to agree on important issues. It was a relationship that was to stand them in good stead in the months ahead. AWS arranged to meet Symonds for lunch on 1 April and told him about his plans. Symonds readily agreed to join AWS.

Symonds had shared AWS's reservations about the ambitious but foolhardy plan to introduce new technology into *The Daily Telegraph*. After years in the doldrums, the newspaper had decided in 1984 to leap thirty to fifty years ahead in production technology and bring in photocomposition and web-offset printing at new plants in Manchester and London's Docklands. Contracts worth £100 million were signed without the necessary finance being in place and redundancy payments of £48 million agreed. Symonds realised that the newspaper would not be able to service its debt and wondered why the management had not opted for printing at satellite plants around Britain. During the course of his co-produc-tion of the employment survey with AWS, he had realised that the only way to achieve something in newspapers was to do it yourself. When AWS approached him he thought: 'If Eddie Shah can raise the money why can't we?'

Symonds believed that there was a chance to do something different from the existing players. He realised that at the quality end of the market, little attention was being given to the structured marketing of the product. Having joined *The Daily Telegraph* in his late twenties, he felt that the newspaper had limited appeal for younger readers and had done nothing to correct its venerable image. Without at that stage having the benefit of any specially-commissioned market research into their projections, he felt instinctively that there lay a fertile field ready to be ploughed and harvested outside the marbled mausoleum of *The Daily Telegraph's* Fleet Street building.

While proceeding with preliminary work into the possible new paper, AWS on the other track was consolidating his plan to save *The Daily Telegraph*. On 14 May 1985 he sent a memorandum to Lord Hartwell which contained a proposal to raise additional equity capital through a Business Expansion Scheme offer to readers.

He wrote: 'Securing additional capital in this way would, I believe, increase the attraction of our current offer of preferred ordinary shares to the City institutions and reduce the amount of lease and debt finance that we require. As we already have a draft prospectus prepared, such a plan could be put into operation quickly.

'Apart from extra capital, a successful BES offer would bring us the additional advantage of substantially strengthening our rapport with our readers.' He pointed out that if a mere 1 per cent of *The Telegraph's* readership of 1.2 million put up £500 each (the minimum sum which qualified for tax relief) £6 million would be raised; if 5 per cent, or 60,000 people did, £30 million would be raised.

He then explained in detail the tax situation concerning such a BES scheme and concluded: 'In addition, a share option scheme should be set up for senior executives. In this way a unity of purpose would be established between readers, City institutions, staff and management. We should then be entitled to feel every confidence in the future of *The Daily Telegraph*.'

His plans and his confidence fell on deaf ears. Lord Hartwell thought that readers should not be mixed up with investors; AWS believed differently – he felt that if the paper had to lose control it was better to lose it to readers than to a tycoon. He said later that had his rescue plan been adopted he probably would have dropped his desire to start a new paper.

Seven months later the inevitable happened, Lord Hartwell had to concede that control of the newspaper, which had been in the hands of his family for 57 years, had been passed over to Conrad Black, the Canadian businessman. Ironically, the decision to move over to new technology had spelled the death-knell for Lord Hartwell. The newspaper lost £16 million between April and September and its bankers lost confidence in its management. Black eventually paid £30 million for half the shares in the company. It was against this background that AWS continued to lay his financial plans.

Meanwhile his team was quietly growing. In April, Symonds asked Douglas Long, who retired in 1984 as chief executive of Mirror Group Newspapers who publish the *Daily Mirror, Sunday*

Mirror and *Sunday People*, if he would be interested in giving them the benefit of many years' experience at the sharp business and production end of the newspaper market. He was taken on by the project and began to get involved. In May a third journalist, Stephen Glover, a feature and leader writer at *The Daily Telegraph*, was approached and asked to join AWS and Symonds. Glover, who had known Symonds from their student days at Oxford, had persuaded him in 1981 to leave the *Financial Times* to join *The Daily Telegraph*. He had a passing acquaintance with AWS from their occasional meetings in editorial conferences. Glover was intrigued by the prospects, and after meeting AWS at his home in June, agreed to become a partner in the venture.

Glover was to say later: 'It is important to remember at that stage the type of newspaper that they envisaged was very different from what we ended up with. Following the early indications from Saatchi and Saatchi, they were planning a paper that would appeal to younger people and one that was full of colour – possibly ten to sixteen pages of colour in two sections. The editorial tempo was far more downmarket.' Glover felt that what was needed was perhaps a new version of *The Daily Telegraph* which would appeal to a new generation of young people just as *The Telegraph* had done for young people in the 1930s.

From then until September, the three or four founders met once or twice a week to discuss projections and to do calculations based on costings gleaned from *The Daily Telegraph* and the *Daily Mirror*. There were several meetings with Perriss who was able to steer them onto the right course when it came to advertising and marketing projections.

Symonds wrote editorial papers about what the possible content should be. He was very keen on a heavy emphasis on news analysis, the arts and going out. In August AWS wrote a paper which detailed his objectives – to produce a daily broadsheet paper; to aim at the ABC1 category in terms of readers; readers should be aged 25 to 44; these readers should make up 50 per cent of the total readership; by using new technology to the fullest extent, the break-even point of such a newspaper, with eight pages of colour, might be 320,000 copies which could be achieved by getting 15 per cent of *The Daily Telegraph* readers and 10 per cent each from the *Daily Mail*, the *Daily Express*, *The Times* and *The Guardian*; funding such a project would cost around £20 million.

AWS returned from holiday on 2 September having sketched out this first business plan. By that stage the three journalists and Long had agreed that they must 'go for it'. The timing was right, to delay would be to lose the opportunity which, by then, they were more convinced than ever would work.

On 16 September they had a crucial meeting with Saatchi who agreed to back the project on a 'no foal, no fee basis'. They would undertake proper market research but if the paper failed, they would not charge the founders. From then on the founders committed themselves far more to the project.

The first formal research then took place. About 1,000 telephone interviews with ABC1 adults were conducted by Research Surveys of Great Britain Ltd, a subsidiary of AGB Research PLC, to see what potential readers in the 25-44-year-old group felt about existing newspapers. The findings then analysed by Saatchi and Saatchi confirmed most of the ideas, hunches and instincts of the founders.

The main results were as follows:

1) That 15 per cent were not completely satisfied with the upmarket newspaper they read and that 11 per cent had considered changing their newspaper.

2) That 30 per cent of those who had changed their newspaper-reading habits had done so in the past by taking an extra newspaper.

3) That more than 80 per cent of the sample preferred a newspaper with no loyalty to any one political party. 49 per cent felt that the national dailies did not offer balanced reporting and that issues were commented on not so much according to their merits as on party lines.

4) That 20 per cent of those interviewed said that they would like more national dailies to choose from.

5) That 35 per cent felt that newsapers tried to appeal to too broad an audience and 20 per cent said that they would be very interested in reading a national newspaper aimed directly at 'people of my own age group doing my sort of job'.

6) That 43 per cent felt that newspapers should complement television and radio news more effectively, by offering more commentary and interpretation than at present.

7) That 29 per cent could not name a daily newspaper which offered a 'well-rounded read with plenty of general interest articles as well as news analysis'.

8) That 38 per cent of the sample believed that national newspapers ought to cover regional news and events, but 84 per cent could not name any national daily newspaper which did so.

They could now proceed with information which confirmed that there was a real demand for a newspaper which offered a combination of news, analysis and entertaining information. It seemed natural that AWS would do the bulk of the financial planning and Symonds and Glover devote their main interest to printing plants, finding premises and discussing the internal office layout with architects. All this time, the project was still secret although their wives knew about and supported the venture. Linda Tanner, AWS's secretary, was also fully involved with the project and was later to prove invaluable in finding the right people to begin raising the money.

The team was growing further with Ron Cotton, former Circulation Director of Mirror Group Newspapers, advising on distribution using traditional methods (AWS: 'The most efficient part of the existing newspaper industry as it is today'). Bill Wrightson, Technical Adviser to Portsmouth and Sunderland Newspapers from 1966 to 1985, was advising the team working on technical and new technological details.

AWS had decided to return to basics and rediscover the essential truths about running a business – it can only succeed if it produces profits efficiently and then distributes them etc; all truisms but a good example of the logical approach behind the set-up of the newspaper. He was soon to get involved with professional financial advisers and investment experts who would test the strength of his business plans to the utmost. His dream was shortly to be laid on the psychologist's couch to be probed and analysed scrupulously before it could be turned into a working and approved project. Later he was to liken the whole experience of setting up the newspaper to crossing 1,000 bridges. Each bridge was a major hurdle in terms of finance, recruitment, technology or circulation. Each one had to be crossed; to falter at one would be to fail.

What's in a name?

Throughout those early months, they still had to make one crucial decision – what was the new newspaper going to be called? In one of his early memos, AWS had referred to an 'independent newspaper' but this description as a possible title did not occur to them until much later. Symonds recalls coming up with the title late in 1985, but until the end of January 1986, the plans were often called Project Arthur, or The Daily Arthur. This refers to Arthur Daly, an unscrupulous used-car salesman who appeared in a British television series called *Minder*. One of his stock phrases was : 'A nice little earner'. Thus, through convoluted syntactical use of English, AWS's scheme was named.

Various names were put up – *The Nation, The Examiner, 24 Hours*. The founders wanted something that would reflect strongly their editorial intent and the new appeal of the newspaper. It had to be marketable, attractive and not used by anyone else.

In January 1986, S & S carried out market research on six possible names – *The Examiner, The Chronicle, The Independent, The Arena, The Nation* and *24 Hours*. The form of the research is fascinating. The team began by asking their sample of 500 people in the right readership target area their preferences for the six titles. Three stood out clearly – *The Examiner* (105 people), *The Chronicle* (102), *The Independent* (101). Less popular were *The Arena* (81), *The Nation* (78) and *24 Hours* (59). In terms of particular likes and dislikes, *The Independent* came first with 64 per cent in favour, followed by *The Examiner* (63%), *The Chronicle* (59%), *24 Hours* (59%), *The Nation* (57%) and *The Arena* (51%).

In terms of the imagery conjured up by the various names, the following 'pen portraits' were drawn up:

The Independent – 'young name; quite left-wing but not unbalanced; reasonably open-minded; no class bias; no bias to the professions or business; reasonable sex bias; good for both single and family people; very strong on modern outlook; strong on for people low regional bias.'

The Examiner – 'older people's name; right-wing; open-minded; strongly upmarket; clearly masculine; both family and single people; business and professional people; strong on for people like me; quite traditional rather than modern; strong southern bias.'

The Chronicle – 'strongly an older people's name; clearly right-wing; not very open-minded; upmarket; masculine; family and both single people; very traditional in outlook; quite high on not for people like me; no strong regional bias.'

The Arena – 'young; not much political bias; open-minded; quite upmarket; strong (relatively speaking) as being for women; for single people; very strong on modern outlook; southern; not bad on for people like me, but matched by not for people like me.'

24 Hours – 'ageless; no political bias; open-minded; no class bias; for both men and women; no family type bias; very strong on modern outlook; good regional spread.'

The Nation – 'good age spread, quite high on 40 +; strongly right-wing; not open-minded; a bit down-market; lowest score on for women; traditional more than modern outlook; imbalance towards not for people like me; good northern appeal.'

The conclusions drawn from the research into imagery were evident and uncompromising: that *The Nation* and *The Chronicle* evoke unfavourable images and that *The Nation* is not very well-liked; that *24 Hours* and *The Arena* while having potential in image terms are not names people feel comfortable with for a daily newspaper; *The Examiner* while appealing conceptually and in imagery terms, generally is a bit more biased towards older, upmarket right-wing men than *The Independent*, which also scores well at a conceptual level; that *The Independent* has good image appeal and would seem to be the best choice.

Thus the name was not born or suddenly dreamed up – it was the product of intensive market research matching the inclinations of most of the founding team. In hindsight, the name seems ideal in editorial terms but perhaps a little cumbersome in marketing and advertising display terms.

In the meantime £2 million had been raised without the benefit of a title for the newspaper.

Mrs Thatcher's visit to Middlesborough in September 1987, her first
inner city initiative. (Photo: John Voos)

2: The Finance

> . . . *O Money, Money! What an Influence hast*
> *thou on all the Affairs of the quarreling, huffing Part of*
> *this World . . . How art Thou . . . the great Wheel in*
> *the vast Machine of Politick Motion, the Vehicle of*
> *Providence, the great Medium of Conveyance, in which all*
> *the Physick of the secret Dispensation in human*
> *Affairs is administered, and by the Quantity of which*
> *it operates to Blessing or Cursing?*
>
> *Daniel Defoe (1661?–1731)*

Dinner parties both began and ended the sequence of fund-raising. The first, on 25 August 1985, was given by AWS's secretary Linda Tanner. Among the guests were Tom Attwood, a partner in Stephen Rose and Partners, a small firm of financial consultants in the City. Linda told Attwood that her boss had an interesting project but she could not go into details. Her caution was well-placed for another guest at the party was a close colleague of AWS at *The Daily Telegraph. The Telegraph* and the world at large were still unaware of his plans.

Three days later over lunch Linda gave Attwood more details about the project. Attwood was intrigued and agreed to meet AWS on 18 September. He listened to AWS's explanation of what he was planning. AWS explained that although he knew a staggering number of people in the City who ran businesses he did not know anyone who knew about starting up a business. Would Stephen Rose and Partners help?

Attwood took away a copy of AWS's first business plan, just five pages of handwritten notes. He recalls that it was very interesting but incomplete: 'There were fairly unsophisticated costings at the back. Funnily enough many of the figures turned out to be extremely accurate after the event.'

His partners back at Stephen Rose agreed that he could research the project further. Attwood again: 'As soon as I intimated that we would try to help him as much as possible all hell broke loose. One was required to work at every hour of the day.'

For his part, it was only Linda's friendship with Attwood that got AWS to explore that approach. He said: 'I was rather unwilling to do it because I had not heard of Stephen Rose and Partners and I have a rather arrogant view that if I haven't heard of people they're not important. In the City if I haven't heard of them, they're bound to be pretty small – and they are.'

It was now the third week in September and Attwood began to set the train in motion. AWS wanted a guide to take him and his project through the City maze. Attwood's first advice was to go for venture capital as opposed to a merchant bank for the finance.

Then Attwood and AWS went to see John Perriss at Saatchi and Saatchi who had been organising the initial market research. The research findings would be vital to help convince investors of the viability of the project. Stephen Rose advised AWS that he should ensure that his advisors at every stage were the best. Attwood: 'He had to go first class, for as a start-up no one had done anything of this magnitude before and Eddie Shah had already found that the City was less than sympathetic.'

At that time AWS had decided that he needed £20 million. Stephen Rose checked his figures and were convinced that he had some sort of proposition. AWS: 'Although I had never heard of them, a second rule came into play, which is to go with the grain. They seemed quite helpful, so I thought I'll stick with these people for a while and see where it leads me. I never felt defenceless. I always felt that I knew so many people in the City that if this route wasn't working I would just ring up one of my many friends.'

Two stages of documentation were suggested to AWS:

1) He would need a well-considered business plan to convince a main merchant bank that it was a business worth sponsoring. (The middle of September was taken up with turning the research data produced by Research Surveys of Great Britain, the subsequent interpretation of those findings by Saatchi and Saatchi and the founders' ideas, into a more formal plan. The target would be the stockbrokers and the merchant bank which would eventually sell the whole deal. In order to make the plan as professional as possible Attwood introduced AWS to Arthur Andersen, the management consultants and accountants, towards the end of September. They agreed to check the projections for a business plan that were being made.)

2) He should produce a prospectus to raise the money.

(A prospectus must demonstrate the reasonableness of a proposal. Investors' protection laws require that all the facts included in the prospectus must be true and that no material matter should be excluded. Material in the sense that if it were there, it would have influenced the investment decision. If you are found guilty of fraud, the penalty is up to 7 years' imprisonment and if you are negligent in the prospectus you are liable to legal action. Usually only merchant banks have the wherewithal to produce documents in defence of a claim of negligence and to prevent fraud. Merchant banks also have the ability to assess plans in a way that is acceptable to the investing institutions.)

Everyone at that stage was aware that there was no real history of raising money for newspapers. Eddie Shah had been given a rough time by one leading merchant bank and eventually ended up raising his launch capital from such esoteric sources as the Hungarian International Bank in London with not a single pension fund or insurance company being involved. His costings looked attractive on paper as did his plan to break the monopoly of the unions and set up an independent distribution system but time would show that he badly miscalculated in several areas of expenditure and preparation.

From mid-September to early October, Stephen Rose were putting together a document that was sufficiently professional to tell AWS's story as well as possible and to convince a merchant bank that it was something worth sponsoring and around which a prospectus could be built. Attwood: 'This was not a sales document in the sense that we were trying to buy and sell shares but it was a sales document in the sense of trying to sell the idea to the merchant banks.'

They had already convinced AWS that he needed a stockbroker first. AWS: 'I was rather surprised at this, I thought I needed a banker.' Stephen Rose suggested de Zoete and Bevan. AWS: 'I thought that's okay, that's in my rule. I'm only going to go for the best people, they're in the top five.'

On 3 October, AWS and Attwood went to see David Porter, a corporate finance director at de Zoete and Bevan. The company later told AWS that they expected Porter to tell him to get lost after half an hour. As it happened, de Zoete were intrigued and asked AWS to make a presentation. Porter said: 'I was very sceptical at first but when Andreas explained the decision to have separate production and printing, I was taken with the idea.'

AWS said later: 'I'd never done a presentation before. Every step, every day, I learnt something completely new.' The presentation was given on 8 October; also present was Johnnie Townsend, a senior partner in sales at de Zoete, who was later to be instrumental in helping raise the money. It lasted a couple of hours and was to be the first of many over the next six months. It was partly based on Project Arthur which was research presented by Saatchi and Saatchi on 16 September. That research was taken on by Stephen Rose and used as source material for the working document.

The all-important document had been written in two weeks, including one particularly gruelling weekend at the end of September. As the project became more and more real in their minds and the flower slowly opened, a sense of urgency which was to stay with the founders until launch and long after, became the natural order of days and nights. They knew then the raising of the money would have to be done in two parts—some to get the company moving in terms of renting a building and ordering machinery and the rest when the plans had been more formalised.

The entire process was a fusion of skills and interests; on the one hand the entrepreneurial amateurs AWS, Symonds and Glover who, for example, had come up with staff costs on a broad base of one year; on the other hand, Stephen Rose and his colleagues who were highly experienced at balance sheets and spreadsheets. They turned AWS's initial figures into monthly cash flows and profit-and-loss projections for up to five years ahead. AWS and his co-founders were asked to sit down and be more diligent about exactly what the costs were going to be and why. And the costs themselves – how could one be precise and accurate about something as elusive as a successful newspaper?

Stephen Rose based a lot of their calculations on the suggested circulation from Saatchi and Saatchi. They used market data on existing volumes of advertising and pricing from other leading titles and discounted those by a significant amount in order to guesstimate what the advertising revenue might be. It was the key factor. With a projected and aimed-for small circulation, revenue from the cover price would initially provide a relatively small income but advertising revenue would determine the success or failure of the project. At the end of September 1985 a circulation of 400,000 was predicted for October 1987 (the actual figure was 372,231).

The Independent was then, and is now, expensive in terms of journalists' salaries, expenses and costs, but they provide the raw material which sells the product. The costs – numbers, salaries – were worked out on the basis of *The Daily Telegraph* and the *Daily Mirror*. It was essential to get those figures right. Attwood: 'Investors will forgive you if your analysis of the market place is wrong or if you fail to achieve the market penetration but they will never forgive you if you get wrong something that is more stable than that – how many people, how much the computer equipment will cost etc.'

It is an inexact science but there are many aspects of the business that you are expected to get right.

Progress was made. de Zoete and Bevan agreed to act as stockbrokers to the new venture. On 11 October, AWS was advised by his new stockbrokers to try two merchant banks, Kleinwort Benson and Charterhouse Japhet who AWS saw on 16 October. AWS's preference was for Kleinwort's but eventually, for unexplained reasons, the bank rejected his overtures. Charterhouse Japhet joined the movement on 12 November. It was yet another important step for AWS because Charterhouse had a better history of successes in the venture capital market than others. Bruce Fireman, the bank's corporate finance director, agreed to sponsor the issue subject to various conditions:

1) That a proper business plan be completed.

2) That he carry out a 'due diligence test' on that business plan. That meant he and his colleagues checking all the statements for error, even visiting the print plants to check out tentative agreements. Fireman explained, much to the dismay of Stephen Rose and Partners and AWS and his co-founders, that he would need all of November and probably December too to complete his work.

3) That a finance director be appointed.

By then they thought they needed £18 million for the entire operation – £2 million for the first stage and £16 million for the second. Stephen Rose would raise the £2 million from aggressive risk-takers. The first round of finance was needed to put down a deposit rental of several months on the building where the entire newspaper would eventually be housed. Advance payments would have to be made for the £5 million worth of computer equipment that was needed. And this first tranche had to be completed by 7 January 1986, or the building they had set their sights on, 40 City Road, would be leased by the landlords, Commercial Union Properties, to somebody else. The cost of organising a full prospectus would also be very high.

Attwood and his fund-raisers knew that their 'sporting investors' would be happy that Charterhouse Japhet were doing the stringent 'due diligence test' and that they would hand over the cheques as soon as that task had been completed. But the timing was once again crucial if yet another brick was to be cemented into place.

They all set to work trying to balance the breakeven figure on circulation with the amount of money they needed to raise. The most important principle was as follows: Either there was a positive gap in the market or a negative one.

Perhaps the key document was a Christie diagram produced by S & S which showed first the position of newspapers in the market in terms of their readers, then superimposed on that, the buying practices, and therefore economic strengths and power, of the younger generation. It showed, for example, that *The Daily Telegraph* had a predominantly older readership which did not spend much on the type of goods and services that there was a very large market for among the affluent new young sector. The diagram showed that it was expensive for advertisers to reach younger, better-off people. They did not watch much commercial television and while in absolute terms many read *The Daily Telegraph*, an advertiser buying space in it for, say a foreign holiday programme, had to pay for even more readers who only took their holidays in Eastbourne. There was an advertising gap and a circulation gap. Hence the so-called yuppie paper was born.

Fireman believes that those figures really sold the entire thing. Still, business wisdom was cautious – 'There may be a gap in the business but is there a business in the gap?' S & S convinced the doubters by affirming that if you produce the product to fill the gap, the advertising and the revenue will follow.

Throughout this period – November and December 1985 – only four people were directly working on the business plan, taking it to pieces, examining its component parts and putting it back together again – Fireman and two colleagues from Charterhouse Japhet and Attwood from Stephen Rose. AWS was to prove a hard taskmaster, ringing up several times a day to check progress. Attwood: 'He would ask what have you achieved today, and what do we need to achieve tomorrow.' The Commercial Union was still restless and wanted to rent the building at 40 City Road to another client. They were persuaded shortly before Christmas 1985 to wait.

As Fireman and his team continued their 'due diligence test' they came across mathematical infelicities made by S & S which had to be corrected if the business plan and later the prospectus were to have any chance of standing up to scrutiny. One example was S & S's prediction that the new newspaper would attract three readers per copy. They actually meant 2.7 but the figures had been rounded up, which meant, in this case, that the difference of .3 was a shortfall of 10 per cent in advertising revenue or some £2 million a year.

Attwood, ever more conscious of the need to maintain the momentum, was pursuing his 'sporting investors'. He met Newmarket Venture Capital and made a presentation with AWS soon afterwards. They agreed to put money in. Attwood, AWS and the whole enterprise were gathering speed. After Newmarket came Touche Remnant. Then Henderson Administration, Murray Ventures, Framlington and finally the development wing of Charterhouse itself. Six presentations were made to six investors and all six agreed to come in. AWS: 'It was a 100 per cent hit ratio.'

It was a remarkable and unprecedented achievement. The normal practice is for a prospectus to be sent out first; the investors had nothing but a presentation, a business plan and the assurance that a merchant bank would eventually help to produce a prospectus and raise the second tier of finance.

Personnel was still a key issue. Douglas Long was appointed managing director and Christopher Barton, the finance director of Portsmouth and Sunderland Newspapers, was approached through the executive search firm Korn Ferry and asked to become finance director. He eventually agreed to resign and join the new company when the £2 million was raised and paid over.

Meanwhile the hard-kept secret was about to be revealed. On 22 December 1985, *The Sunday Times* printed a story saying that a 'mysterious band of newspaper editors and executives' were trying to raise £30 million to start a new national daily newspaper. Five days later the cat was out of the bag when on Friday, 27 December, the *Financial Times* ran an article that revealed more details and named the founders. The game was up. AWS saw Lord Hartwell and Symonds and Glover saw Bill Deedes, the Editor of *The Telegraph*, and they all left the newspaper on 28 December. Their ambitious plans were public knowledge and they were now able to conduct their business openly from the offices in London Wall where they moved on 30 December.

A crucial meeting was held at Charterhouse on 7 January with the six investors, AWS's team, Attwood and Fireman. It was the culmination of the previous few weeks of intense negotiation, appeals and checking. The six agreed to put in roughly £400,000 each. There was still no prospectus but Fireman had completed his 'due diligence test' and pronounced in favour of the plan. They bought £2 million of equity ultimately because the proposals were so good that they were convinced there was a business there to invest in.

The champagne flowed. The building was secure. The finance director came on board. The advances on the computer equipment were sorted out and the professional fees could be paid.

But there was no respite. The prospectus had to be finished in order to raise the £16 million needed to launch the newspaper. If the second round of finance was not raised the original investors would lose everything.

The prospectus had to contain all the material facts. Omissions either through fraud, negligence or ignorance could result in heavy legal action. So two firms of solicitors were drafted in to ask each other searching questions. From 7 January to mid-February, hard and fast work went into the first draft of the prospectus which was produced by Charterhouse. Every item was checked and verified.

At the same time the search was on to find a suitable chairman for the fledgling company. None of the founders had run a company and that lack of experience would not go down well with the institutional investors they were seeking millions from. Someone was needed who could provide a background of sound business practice and experience and who was of high standing in the business and investment community.

A shortlist was drawn up with attention being concentrated on the retail sector and consumer businesses. Lord Sieff of Brimpton, who gave up the chairmanship of Marks and Spencer in 1984 after 12 years and is now its president, more than adequately answered the essential criteria. He was selected as the best choice from a small shortlist. Lord Sieff met AWS at the beginning of January and after some hesitation agreed to become non-executive chairman as soon as the second round of financing was complete. What attracted him most to the idea, bearing in mind his own outstanding record of staff participation and good relations between management and workers at M & S, was the intention to allow everyone on the staff of the proposed newspaper to become shareholders.

He also liked the way the prospectus was being drawn up with the elements of risk defined and assessed. His appointment of chairman on 17 April 1986, gave the company its seal of approval. Here was a chairman who could correct the level of inexpertise at the head of the company. After Lord Sieff, two other non-executive directors were appointed: Ian Hay Davidson (managing partner of Arthur Andersen & Co, the chartered accountants, from 1966 to 1982, and from 1983 to 1986, deputy chairman and chief executive of Lloyd's of London) and George Duncan (chairman of Lloyds Bowmaker Finance Ltd and a director of Lloyds Bank plc).

Before the final prospectus was completed on 3 April 1986, a 'red herring' prospectus was prepared. It was a draft version sent out with the promise that the final prospectus would not be materially different.

It went to existing clients of Stephen Rose, Charterhouse Japhet and de Zoete and Bevan, and their salesmen began the final surge to raise the money. Back-up documents were prepared in case prospective investors had further questions or required further details of all the checks that had been made. The follow-up presentations began in earnest on 28 February.

The documentation having been done it was now up to AWS and

his fellow directors and advisers to sell the idea to sceptical investment managers and analysts who might have initial doubts about the success of a new newspaper.

The structure of the second round of finance was different from the first in that it had to take loan stock as well as equity into account. The overall ratio determined was £10 million of equity and £8 million of loan capital. A million of equity was allotted to the founders – 10 per cent. The first round investors put up £2 million for 2 million ordinary shares. The founders put in £130,000 with AWS contributing about 40 per cent of that. Their allocation was as follows: £100,000 for 1 million ordinary shares and £30,000 for 3 million convertible shares.

AWS and Adrian O'Neill, Advertising and Marketing Director, who had joined the company on 1 January from a similar position on *TV Times* magazine, attended 100 per cent of the presentations, Douglas Long, managing director, about 90 per cent and Christopher Barton about 30 per cent along with a salesman or team from de Zoete and someone from the bank. The presentations were scheduled to last for 45 minutes but often lasted twice as long as that, so intense was the interest. The bulk were in London with two trips to Scotland. Sometimes, important working dinners were given at the Garrick Club in London for between 8 to 10 very senior people in the fund management companies they had approached.

In all, about 100 investors were approached and 60 presentations were made. David Porter recalled later that, after the dispute at Rupert Murdoch's News International newspaper plant at Wapping had begun in January, newspapers and their future were very much news themselves. The sales team from de Zoete had to convince the potential investors that there would not be the same union problems and the new paper had the ability to attract readership and circulation. The newspaper's editorial profile, marketing strategy and advertising prospects were put forward. Costings of salaries, computer equipment, the price of newsprint and office furniture were revealed and justified. Searching questions came back from the assembled analysts. The central query was Why? not How? 'Why was there a gap in the market?' 'Why was a circulation of so-and-so predicted?' They were not going to invest unless their doubts were removed. Porter again: 'It took a long time to work out the production side of things. There was a high element of questions about the new technology and would it work. A lot of investors also looked very carefully at how the management would be remunerated.'

AWS stood up well to the pressure of travelling around and giving the same presentation over and over again. After the first few, he and his fellow presenters knew which questions to expect and had the answers ready. Not too glib and not too quick, but the answers were there. AWS's grasp of the issues involved was second to none. It was his project, he had nurtured it from the start and nothing would allow him to be swayed from his path. His serene

The front cover of the prospectus for Newspaper Publishing plc, the company which runs *The Independent* – April 1986.

manner and lofty presence worked in his favour. Nothing seemed to worry him or allow him to display undue emotion.

He was accused once or twice of avoiding looking his audience in the eye. 'Use more eye contact', one of his advisers told him. Whatever his public technique was, it worked. Thirty of those companies approached, agreed eventually to invest in the new project. The maximum equity allowed was 10 per cent, a safeguard to prevent the company being controlled by a single investor.

By March, many investors were still deciding. Some had said no and a lot had yet to say yes. Porter was conscious of time running out and the de Zoete team under Townsend were constantly chasing people up. By 10 April, the team were becoming increasingly exhausted. All the money had been raised apart from a few hundred thousand pounds from 30 institutional investors, ranging from the Prudential and the Legal and General assurance companies to the Post Office pension fund and South Yorkshire County Council. The core group of advisers decided enough was enough, the business had to start otherwise targets would not be met. Bruce Fireman said he would underwrite the issue but in the event it was not necessary.

For de Zoete it had been a novel experience in terms of exposure in the newspapers. Porter was used to similar fund-raising ventures being kept under wraps. In this case such was the press interest that many details were instantly reported.

AWS was to say later: 'I had two advantages, the second springs out of the first: you could only put this together if you were a financial journalist because only a financial journalist would, I think, have the confidence to think he could raise the money. The second advantage was that I was quite often able without any problem to go to the top.'

Including the first round, £18 million had been invested in a brief few months – the biggest sum ever raised on the venture capital market for a single and new enterprise. On 17 April, the cheques had been received. *The Independent* was literally in business. The tired but happy team gathered at Charterhouse for a well-deserved celebratory dinner. The wine and food reflected the elation and light-headedness of the occasion. To drink, Puligny Montrachet 1983, Château Gruaud Larose 1970, Cockburns 1960 and XL Champagne brandy; to eat, L'hommard froid à mon oncle Theodore, Filet de boeuf jardinière à la façon de milord Cooper, Les pommes Ishmailiennes, Scoop de sorbet de champagne avec les mangoes de Jacksonburg, Fraises Boot, Les fromages Stitch, Café Pension Dressler.

AWS wandered over at one stage to Attwood and asked: 'We're doing all right, Tom, aren't we?'

It was a fine understatement.

NB: The success of raising the money was somewhat diluted when it was discovered in July 1986 that Robert Maxwell, ubiquitous publisher of the *Daily* and *Sunday Mirror* and *Sunday People* newspapers, had secretly acquired a 4.81% holding in *The In-*

dependent through a a financial services company called Lancashire and Yorkshire. The last thing the journalists wanted was a 'press baron' to have a stake in the enterprise but they were reassured by the safeguard inherent in the rule disqualifying any individual shareholder from having more than 10 per cent of the equity.

Harold Schmidt and Ed Moses in the final of 400 mm hurdles at the World Championships in Rome, September 1987. (Photo: David Ashdown)

3: The Planning

He who first shortened the labour of copyists
by device of Movable Types was disbanding hired armies,
and cashiering most Kings and Senates, and
creating a whole new democratic world; he had invented
the art of printing.

Thomas Carlyle (1795–1881)

Technology

Newspapermen in Britain, especially journalists, owe a huge debt to Eddie Shah. His drive and determination to challenge the Luddites in Fleet Street, both in management and in the unions, pulled aside the iron curtain that had stifled innovation in printing and typesetting techniques for so long. As we shall see in later chapters, from the early days in newspapers, progress – and often editorial improvement – has been conditioned and governed by technology. Shah invented nothing – the technology had been around for many years, both in typesetting and printing. He became convinced, while running a series of free newspapers mainly used as an advertising medium, that the benefits and control of the so-called new technology should not remain in the hands of the National Graphical Association. The NGA had built up immense power over newspaper owners and managers through the militant use of the 'closed shop' which restricted entry to the production side of newspapers to union members and the 'closed mind' which resisted any forms of new technology.

Until the late 1970s and early 1980s, the traditional method of producing typeset material and turning that into pages was, in simplified terms, as follows – the journalist, either writer or sub-editor, would produce the words for headlines and articles and give them to a compositor who would set the words using an old-fashioned Linotype machine which had scarcely changed for many decades. The metal type produced would then be gathered together by another compositor to make up a page. The completed page would be turned into a plate which would then be laid on a printing press.

Every activity concerning the production of a national news-paper after the article, headline or photograph left the hands of the journalist, was strictly controlled by a member of one of the printing unions who jealously and dogmatically guarded their long-standing monopolistic position. Any attempt by management to change traditional and expensive methods was resisted often by means of a strike that affected or stopped publication. A strike on a newspaper faced with enormous overheads could, and often did, prove ruinous.

After working in the theatre and television, Shah, who was born in Cambridge on 20 January 1940, to a Persian father and English mother, sold his house and bought a newspaper. By 1983, he had six titles in his Messenger Newspaper Group which operated in the Manchester area of England. He expected then a profit of £1 million on a turnover of £5 million – an impressive return. Being relatively new to the world of newspapers and an independent, he had reluctantly accepted the existing practices of union control but found it difficult to swallow any restrictions on his 'right to manage' his company in any way he saw fit.

In July that year, the NGA first used industrial action against him in an effort to control his management. Shah realised that government legislation in the form of the 1980 and 1982 Employment Acts would give him the legal backing he needed to challenge the closed shop; he effectively locked the print unions out of his newspaper plant. He was convinced that he and his non-union people could produce his newspapers. As a 'privateer', Shah seemed to relish the fight which was to be conducted under the eyes of the television cameras and the nation in November that year. The daily scenes of union mobs trying to prevent his newspaper vans leaving his printing plant in Warrington, established ever more firmly in the minds of the politicians, the public and the journalists that the power of unions, especially to restrict the technological advancement and the right to manage in newspapers, should be stopped.

In a political context the ground had been well-prepared by Mrs Thatcher, the Prime Minister, and her Employment Secretary, Norman Tebbit. The legislation aimed at cutting the power of the unions and restoring the right to manage – the two aims seemed synonymous – was tailor-made for one such as Shah, the 'little man' keen to sponsor new jobs locally and independently of any major industrial concerns. By the end of the year he had successfully routed the NGA and become a symbol of freedom against tyranny – an indicator of a deeply-rooted change in political, social and moral values.

Although few newspapers were to follow directly his confrontational tactics to break union monopoly, more and more did make the changeover to new technology after his widely publicised battle. In national terms, the power of the big print unions remained very strong. Britain had witnessed the closure of *The Times* for just under one year between November 1978 and October 1979 because the unions refused to allow the introduction of new typesetting technology and working agreements. The move to computer typesetting or photocomposition by NGA men was to take several more years – it was not until 3 May 1982, that *The Times*, under its new owner, Rupert Murdoch, became the first national newspaper to be set entirely by photocomposition. Although curbs had been made on the power of the unions, their

members still controlled the very heart of newspaper production –
setting the type and controlling the presses.

There was widespread debate in the newspaper industry during
the 1970s and the early 1980s about which was the best way to
achieve the introduction of new technology without losing a newspaper in the process. Confrontation might not work and could
prove extremely expensive. Negotiation seemed pointless – the
print unions wanted to maintain their sole 'right' to set type and
control the entire antiquated machinery that went into newspaper
production and distribution. Of course, their main aim was to
protect the jobs of their members in numbers disproportionately
high in modern terms of productivity. A policy of gradual introduction seemed to emerge. Unions would agree to the introduction of new technology as long as it was not imposed on them. A
string of conditions was laid down – that there would be no compulsory redundancies and that existing terms of voluntary termina-
tion of employment would be maintained.

The principle of double key-stroking came in – that is, that journalists might at some future stage be allowed to use computers to
set or 'key in' their stories but they would then have to be 're-
keyed' by the union compositors. The move to 'single key-stroking' or direct input by the journalists to the computer system
would have to wait, said the unions, unless the managements could
negotiate much more favourable terms for their members. New
printing machinery could be introduced – once again as long as the
unions controlled its use. For years journalists had witnessed the
daily practice of 'Spanish customs', or antiquated privileges used
and abused by the unions; customs that were often the product of
weak and indecisive management in Fleet Street, the traditional
heart of national newspapers.

Shah had broken the mould but for a brief couple of years the
unions were able to reassemble the pieces and fight a rearguard
action. He had also proved to people that the 'agreements' operated
in the Fleet Street area in terms of employment, production and
distribution could be challenged and broken through new technology and strong management. Such was the position after his
victory over the NGA at the end of 1983 and the beginning of 1984.

It was a position that all journalists and newspaper owners or
managers were aware of but none had been able to take his
arguments further and see what the future held. Some would later
reluctantly follow the Shah of Warrington; others would dismiss
him as a troublemaker who could upset their cosy relationship with
the print unions and cause widespread damage; others like *The
Daily Telegraph* would finally realise in 1984 that the way forward
was through new technology but would enter into ruinous
contracts and excessively high redundancy payments for its ageing
workforce.

By March 1985, everyone in the newspaper world knew that the
new technology and the advantages it would bring in terms of
increased efficiency, speed and profits could not be avoided for

long. Yet such was the climate of fear in Fleet Street still, that few believed it could be done on national newspapers without bloody and bitter conflict.

The announcement that month by Eddie Shah that he was going to launch a *new national* newspaper away from Fleet Street, with a low union presence, high profile and direct typesetting input by the journalists, a new and independent form of distribution and the use of web-offset printing, sent a shockwave through newspaper offices. The details which slowly emerged were well-researched and showed that computers lay at the heart of everything – instead of using compositors to make-up pages after the journalists had typeset their copy, why not use electronic page make-up which had existed in parts of Europe and America for some time? And again, instead of having the printing primarily concentrated in Fleet Street and therefore under the control of the unions, why not use modern technology to send pages electronically from the editorial offices, planned to be sited in Westminster, straight to remote or satellite printing plants which were to be set up near major motorway networks?

Modern printing methods could also allow the new newspaper to use colour throughout – until then, with few exceptions, colour in newspapers both for advertisements and for editorial purposes had to be pre-printed, sometimes as much as six weeks ahead of publication. Reporters would be equipped with small personal computers so that they could send their copy direct down a telephone line into the computer system (before then reporters operating away from their home base would telephone their copy to a telephone copy-taker who would type it out, pass it to a journalist for editing and eventual typesetting by a compositor).

Shah had raised a little over £20 million – probably a quarter of the cost to set up and launch a national newspaper by conventional methods. His announcement not only formed Part Two of his single-handed effort to reform the British newspaper industry through breaking the power of the unions but cocked a snoop at existing management in Fleet Street with his single-handed determination to use every aspect of the new technology to take the profitable high ground and keep control over the newspaper. He spoke then about a total staff of 500 people including 300 self-employed local distribution franchise holders. At that time the *Daily* and *Sunday Express* newspapers, one daily selling about 2 million copies and one Sunday selling 2.5 million, had a staff of approximately 6,000 people. His plans and his pioneering words were scoffed at by some. At the time of his announcement he said: ' We're going after an industry that's ripe to be taken, it just needs one guy. And after me there will be more and more people doing their own thing – that's when Fleet Street will really feel the pinch.' A few days later AWS realised the profound importance of what he had proposed.

A few weeks later AWS also knew which way he should proceed in terms of technology and production. Obviously, since his jour-

nalistic experience had always been on the editing or writing side,
his knowledge of up-to-date technology was scarcely comprehen-
sive.

In September 1985 he sought practical help. Bill Wrightson, an
expert on printing, production and new technological systems was
approached and in late October 1985 started work. Although he
agreed with the October 1986 starting date, he felt that the usual
length of time necessary for such a project would be two to three
years.

From 1966 until retiring in April 1985 Wrightson had been
full-time Technical Adviser to Portsmouth and Sunderland Newspapers in Portsmouth where he was involved in the design and
development of Britain's first major computer typesetting and
web-offset colour evening newspaper printing plant.

One of his first major jobs along with the founders was to find
premises suitable for conversion to a modern newspaper office with
regard to department locations, load-bearing of floors, lighting and
ventilation etc. An architect had been found who said that the
conversion would cost £3 million; Wrightson argued, successfully,
that it should cost more like £1 million. The next major task was
the selection of printing plants with special regard to their colour
facilities.

The process, then conducted in secret while the three journalists
were still at work at *The Daily Telegraph*, proved an exacting task.
On one occasion, the founders rang the Telegraph and Argus
group in Bradford, Yorkshire out of the blue, saying: 'Look you
don't know who we are and we're not going to tell you anyway, but
we're thinking about launching a national newspaper. Can we
come and see you?' They said yes. The founders wanted to know
if they had some spare capacity in their printing schedule and what
would be their basic price. AWS: 'We spent two hours with a
director, left his office at 12, went into a pizza place opposite and
emerged a quarter of an hour later having had lunch. I drove while
my two colleagues listened to the radio deciding what the leaders
in *The Telegraph* the next day would be and wrote them in the back
of the car. We ended up in Fleet Street at about half-past two, as
if we'd had a normal day, with the copy written, the articles ready.
We wandered in and said, oh we thought you'd want to write
something about Mr Lawson's economic statement and here it is.'

Less problematical was the choice of typesetting equipment.
The Atex company, part of Eastman Kodak, are the biggest
suppliers of typesetting equipment to newspapers around the
world. Although the basic system had been on the market for some
time, it provided a straightforward and well-defined facility for
journalists. The company was also able to supply the necessary
training and back-up from their base in Leighton Buzzard. In
Wrightson's view, the fact that it was a well-established company
and would not vanish overnight, provided an overpowering
argument.

The production technology of *The Independent* constitutes an important trilogy – direct inputting of text, on-screen layout and facsimile transmissions. It is useful to describe how these three elements work:

Direct input or single key-stroking:

Instead of writers producing their articles on a typewriter and sub-editors checking those articles on paper and then writing the headlines to go with them on paper for typesetting, all these functions can be performed on a VDT or VDU – Visual Display Terminal or Visual Display Unit linked to a mainframe computer. The journalist uses a keyboard which has the normal QWERTY arrangement of the alphabet, as well as special function keys. Instead of paper and roller, the VDTs come with a screen similar to that of a television. Once switched into the computer system, the journalist metaphorically inserts a new piece of paper into the keyboard by opening up a new 'file' which will bear the name of the article and when and where it is being written. As the journalist writes, he or she is able to use a function key to see exactly how long the article is in terms of words, lines or centimetres. Like other word-processing systems, the journalist is able to search for certain words electronically or change words throughout the article by pushing a few keys.

Until the explosive growth from the early 1970s onwards in the use and scope of computer systems in newspapers (mainly in the United States and not in Britain), journalists had relied on paper-work for the bulk of their information. Copy from the major wire news agencies such as Reuters, the Press Association or the United Press International (UPI) came through a wire machine as 'hard copy' and was then cut and pasted onto another sheet of paper or rewritten into an article by a journalist. Nowadays, newspapers all over the world, but still only a few in Britain, can receive all this information via telephone lines directly into a computer. Using an integrated system with the right software, a journalist can call that information from agencies or telexes onto his screen and, to use the standard terminology, cut and paste it onto an existing story or rewrite it. By using the 'split-screen' technique, the journalist can see different stories side by side on different parts of the screen.

Not only can such a system be used for 'word-processing' or 'typesetting' articles or headlines, it can also be used to produce statistical tables and typographical artwork. For example, logos or headlines can be produced with white type on a black background or grey type on a white background with different size rules top and bottom etc. This graphic function seems to be little used by news-papers who prefer to stick to more conventional means of produc-ing artwork.

Again headlines have traditionally been written on pieces of paper which would be typeset by a compositor before being placed onto a page for make-up or composition. Since the birth of printed matter, the editor or sub-editor had counted the letters or charac-ters of a headline or caption or even, at times, a story, to see if it

New technology at work at *The Independent*: On the left is the VDT for text subbing and, on the right, the GT68 terminal for on-screen layout.
(Photo: Herbie Knott)

would fit across the width allowed for it on the page. With a newspaper system such as Atex, sub-editors can write headlines on screen to a predetermined width and type size and the computer will show in seconds if that headline fits or how much it is over or under the requisite width.

Another function of such a paperless system, but one not confined to newspapers, is the use of electronic mail. Letters, memos or urgent messages can be sent to anyone using a VDT in the building in seconds or down telephone lines to anyone with reciprocating equipment anywhere in the world.

Unlike other word-processing software used on personal computers, the journalist can send the finished story or headline to any other journalist working in the building or leave it in the memory of the system where it can later be retrieved by a sub-editor. Or the story can be sent straight to the typesetters in the system to produce a galley (or column) of type or a bromide, a waxed piece of photographic paper used for pasting onto a page.

On-screen full page make-up:

The basic decision to opt for the method was taken early on. It was the natural progression in electronic newspaper production and other associated systems such as electronic archive storage and retrieval and Teletext. Full page make-up had been in use around the world, but particularly in the United States, for a number of years. Without on-screen page make-up, further editorial and technical development would be reduced. At the time of writing, *The Independent* is the only national broadsheet daily to use full page electronic make-up. The tabloid *Today*, now no longer owned by Eddie Shah, also uses an on-screen page make-up system.

Traditionally the design of a page is conducted in the following way. While a journalist is writing or editing an article or headline, the editor in charge of a particular page, be it sports or home news, will be thinking about how to place those stories on that page in relationship to the photographs and advertisements. He will then draw up a layout to show the positioning of the stories, according to merit and importance, the pictures, the captions and the advertisements etc.

The page designer then passes the scheme or layout to a compositor to be 'made up'. I have described how in the days of 'hot metal', stories and headlines were cast in metal and then formed into blocks of type to make up a page which would be turned into a curved plate for positioning on a press. With computer typesetting, the galleys or bromides of the text, headlines and pictures are pasted onto a sheet of paper to make up a page.

The next step was on-screen page make-up where the sketch of the page is reproduced onto a screen with spaces allocated electronically to text, headlines, rules, pictures, graphics and advertisements. All the editorial or advertising material is then sent electronically to the new 'page file' that has been created. Minutes later the content of the entire page is typeset on typesetters attached to

Old technology: A Fleet Street compositor sets metal type on a Linotype machine. (Photo: Herbie Knott)

the main computers. A full-size bromide, or galley, with all the constituent elements – headlines, type etc – is produced for subsequent transfer to the press. To describe it another way, the page make-up processes that traditionally had been done by the craft unions of Fleet Street and the rest of Britain, either by 'hot-metal' or 'cold type' methods, are done electronically to mathematically precise definitions on a computer layout (see chapter 7). The methods of direct inputting of copy by journalists and the ability to make-up pages on-screen has cut dramatically the time it takes to produce a newspaper ready for the presses. It is difficult to quantify, but the editorial production cycle is roughly two-thirds quicker than other methods and the number of people involved in the production of a single page has been reduced from about twenty to five.

In January 1986 Wrightson arranged a visit to Paris to see the offices of the *International Herald Tribune* which had been using Atex equipment for single key-stroking by journalists for several years and had also been in the forefront of transmitting completed pages via satellite to printing centres in different locations around the world. The visit, which was partly a public relations exercise, was the first time AWS met Steve Conaway and Chris Hugh-Jones who were in charge of the computer and technical side of the 'Trib's' operation. Wrightson had decided that he did not want a full-time position on *The Independent* and took the opportunity to sound out Conaway and Hugh-Jones about joining the new newspaper. Initially they were both sceptical but later, convinced by the viability of the project, left their jobs and joined *The Independent* in May 1986 – Conaway as Director of Operations and Hugh-Jones as Data Systems Controller.

At the time they joined, most of the decisions had been taken about the hardware and software for the computer and technical systems. It was thought at the time that the Atex system would not be capable of producing a whole page of news material on-screen and that a system which could handle both type and graphics was needed. The plans, for a system other than Atex, were unscrambled by Conaway and Hugh-Jones after they found that the necessary software for full-page layout was not available and that the mooted Pagemaster system produced by Zenotron could only reproduce digitally pictures onto a page that were no bigger than four inches by six inches. However Zenotron Image-setters married to the Atex system were retained to typeset the pages.

Instead, Conaway opted for the Atex page layout system using a VDT called the GT68. This came in two packages – one for classified advertising make-up and one for news layout, but the American design seemed unsophisticated in British newspaper layout terms. The system had been developed by Jonathan Seybold, the 'guru' of desk-top publishing, in the mid-1970s on the *Minneapolis Star Tribune* in Minnesota, America. Pages had been produced on this system since 1981 but *The Independent* remains the only broadsheet newspaper in Europe to produce the entire product through Atex, apart from an occasional publication in Frankfurt.

It was a profoundly risky option, but Conaway, faced with the philosophical editorial commitment to a system which was not in use, decided that it could be developed and be made operational by October 1986. The system that was supplied was basically a template. All the precise requirements of the newspaper – from the size of the page to the typography of the body type or articles – had to be programmed into the system. Horse-racing tables and crosswords had to be input. Although it was the first full page structure Conaway had worked on, he devised ways 'to get round the system' to meet the editorial requirements. About 1,500 formats (or commands for the computer to follow) were written, of which about 800 primarily reflected the design of the newspaper in layout terms and were written by Philip Hollingbery (see chapter 7). The rest of the formats concerned the text input by journalists, the operation of the mainframe computers themselves and a host of ancillary functions.

Along with the basic format writing, Conaway and his team had to devise highly-complicated back-up mechanisms. Safety networks are vital in mass production for a daily newspaper so reliant on a specific form of typesetting and page layout. If a computer disc fails, there must be a way to save and retrieve the data stored on that disc which might contain all the ingredients of several pages of the newspaper. As one part of the mainframe computers became overloaded, a system had to be devised, particular to the newspaper's need, to cross-flow data to another part which was temporarily unused.

Page transmission:

The third most important technological advance used by *The Independent* is the facsimile transmission of completed pages of the newspaper to the remote printing sites contracted to print the newspaper at launch: Sittingbourne in Kent, Portsmouth in Hampshire, Bradford in Yorkshire and Peterborough in Cambridgeshire.

The machines used are Datrax laser scanning equipment from Crosfield Electronics which basically 'read' a finished page and then translate it into a series of numbers which can be transmitted down a British Telecom Megastream landline, at a rate of one million numbers per second, to a Datrax receiving unit at the printing plants. The receiver reconverts the numbers by using laser beams to punch onto a carbon-coated polystyrene sheet of paper the image of the finished page before it is used to make plates for the press. This system enables two pages to be reproduced many miles away from the newspaper's office a mere 90 seconds after they have been sent.

This technology is comparatively new and made Conaway extremely worried. He said later: 'I was scared about the instability of these devices so I made sure that the installations were perfect, with proper air conditioning and clean, sealed rooms complete with filters.'

The Datrax equipment is also used to send colour separations of advertisements or editorial illustrations which are then reassembled at the printing works. The special Megastream lines are a comparatively rare example of the efficiency of the BT system but, mainly because they are used by the Ministry of Defence, they can be serviced virtually instantly and have caused little trouble to the operation of the newspaper since launch.

The technical side of producing pictures and graphics caused a few problems at first. The original plan was to scan photographs, graphics and advertisements through the computer system into the typesetters in order to output a totally complete page produced by computers ready for transmission to the printing works. However, the time taken and the limitation on picture size proved insurmountable at that stage in late summer 1986. It was decided, in the weeks before launch, to use the Autokon 1000 scanners that had been supplied with the Zenotron equipment to produce bromides or waxed prints of illustrations which could then be pasted onto a page where predetermined spaces had been left for them.

Conaway and his team were faced with huge technical problems over hardware, software, provision of power and wiring, telephone lines and structural building changes in the months between May and October 1986. The first hardware or computer equipment arrived in the third week of June and by the last week in July, the system was functioning to a certain degree. The imagesetters were running by the end of July and the very first test page layout was run through by the end of the first week in August. It is remarkable to realise that four weeks later completed dummy newspapers were being produced under this state-of-the-art system.

Conaway had to retain a cool head as the crucial deadlines came and went. He said later: 'We were conscious of the 7 October deadline all the time. We had to pick and choose what projects could be worked on based on the fact that the newspaper had to be produced. Two weeks before the start I was confident that there would be no problems. One week before launch I felt that the whole thing would go very easily as the faults became predictable and the system began to go faster. But we did ignore the human factor a bit.

'Panic and fear began to hit some people who had been tolerant until the last week. There was mass panic with the number of faults and calls for assistance multiplied by a factor of 10 in the last week. We should have reassured everyone that everything was okay.'

For Conaway, with many years' experience in the newspaper and computer industry, it was more than just another job: 'I had a rule. I had to do it by 7 October without question. It would have been a major personal disaster and there was never any choice for anyone. Any delay would have been translated to the technical department.'

It was a pioneering achievement and remarkable from a

philosophical viewpoint. Journalists of *The Independent*, through the efforts of the three founders, have more power over what they do, and can do, than on any other national newspaper in the world; but they have less knowledge of how it is done than at any time in history. It was comparatively easy to understand how an old-fashioned Linotype machine operated and how a page was assembled and printed. Such is modern technology that few, apart from a technological elite, can begin to understand the inner workings of a computer or facsimile transmitter. The workings of the 'new tech' revolution are a mystery to most people and will become increasingly so as science makes geometric advances in its technological applications. It is a curiously passive acceptance.

Gilbert and George having tea with Mrs Phyllis Till at the Market Cafe, Spitalfields in June 1987. (Photo: Herbie Knott)

4: The Planning

*You cannot hope,
to bribe or twist,
thank God! the
British journalist.
But, seeing what
the man will do
unbribed, there's
no occasion to.*

Humbert Wolfe (1886–1940)

The Journalists

One of the central tenets of the making of *The Independent* was to
go for the best staff in every area of the company. Another was not
to let the excitement and benefits of new technology get in the way
of good journalism and professional writing.

One of Eddie Shah's mistakes was to underestimate the importance of some of his journalists. It is a truism that he decided to
ignore – that a national daily newspaper must have national daily
trained journalists. There are many fine journalists working on
provincial weekly, evening and morning newspapers. The best or
most ambitious of them reach Fleet Street or a national newspaper
fairly early on in their career; most stay there until retirement,
seduced by the excitement, seedy glamour and high remuneration.
Some return disillusioned to their journalistic roots or leave the
profession altogether.

Once Fleet Street as a geographical location is reduced to
housing possibly one newspaper during the next few years and the
benefits of new technology and higher pay spread to newspapers
outside the capital, it remains to be seen whether national newspapers will attract the same quality of journalists that, by and large,
they have done in the past.

One of the few links that *The Independent* has with the old Fleet
Street is the fact that most of its journalists had worked in it before
joining the newspaper. Many of them jumped on board to escape
the remnants of the antiquated ways, practices and union monopolies. Many were doing what the founders had done but from a
different perspective – they were challenging the old order by believing in a new order which was still to be proved.

The very first appointments at *The Independent* dictated themselves – it was natural that AWS would be Editor, Matthew
Symonds, Deputy Editor, and Stephen Glover, Foreign and Assis-

tant Editor. They carried the project until the leak was sprung in the *Financial Times* on 27 December 1985. It was impossible to approach anyone until the project became official, but for some months during the late summer and autumn, considerable thought had been given to staffing the various departments of the newspaper.

The first journalist to ask for a job – on 29 December – was John Torode, then a leader writer of long-standing on *The Guardian*. He eventually became Policy Editor and Chief Leader-writer on the new paper.

In the days that followed as more became known about the new paper, journalists began to prick up their ears, dust off their consciences and . . . examine their bank balances. 'Politically,' said AWS at the end of December, 'it will be non-aligned. The paper will not have a specific party label. It will be somewhere around the centre, but between us we have vigorous views on economic and foreign affairs and home policy.'

It was an important statement for some disaffected but successful journalists. At that time *The Daily Telegraph* was perceived by many journalists to be dull, conventional and right-wing. *The Guardian* was seen by some as dull, conventional and too left-wing. *The Times* was seen by some as dull, conventional and too right-wing. The mood was ripe for change for many journalists who themselves usually fall into one of four categories:

1) Those who are not concerned much by either the political line of their newspaper or the country. They see their job as a professional commitment to produce the best they can for their newspaper. They may move from job to job and from left-wing newspaper to right-wing newspaper and back again seeking career advancement – and more money.

2) Those who are constantly disturbed by the (usually right-wing) policies of their newspaper but realise after a while that they are unable to do anything about it. They often get heavily involved in the journalists' union branch at the newspaper and sometimes in political activities outside it. They are often young and at the start of their journalistic careers.

3) Those who treat the whole practice of journalism as something of a joke – a joke they have played on the editor who employed them. They live by their wits – and by their expense accounts. Very often they are able to produce convincing stories but which, on closer examination, are not worth the floppy disc they are written on.

4) Those who are concerned about the policies and politics of their newspapers but are content to accept most things apart from proprietorial interference in their work. They are often highly-experienced and, despite any disillusion about the newspaper, will have carved themselves a respectable niche with a respectable salary and will only move after much deliberation unless desperate.

Most journalists, however, have a healthy regard for the failures and problems of Fleet Street. As the principles clarified in state-

Title pieces: Some of the many mastheads designed for the newspaper.

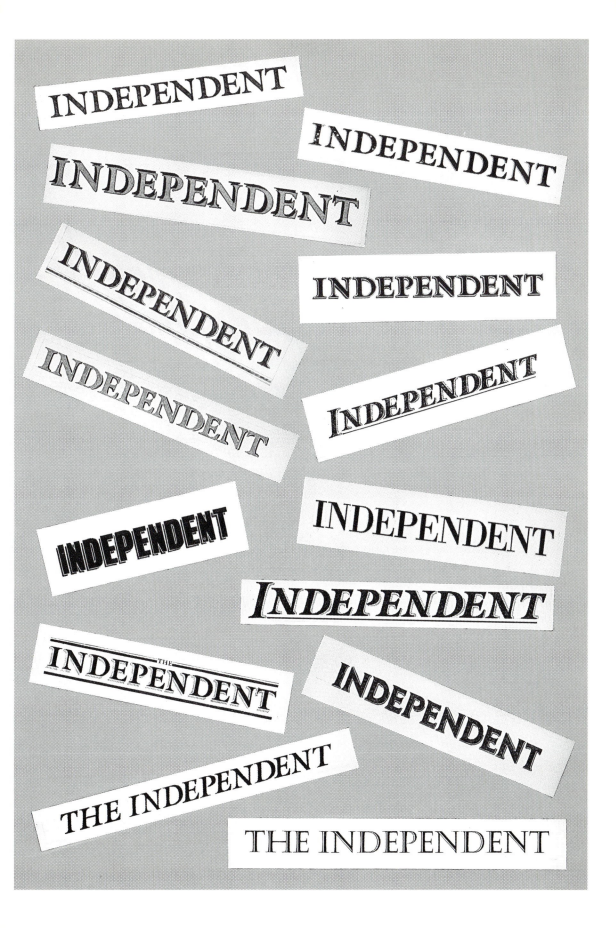

ments made early in January the new newspaper seemed almost too good to be true:

On economic issues, it would advocate free market solutions.

On social issues, it would take a liberal line.

On foreign issues, it would be pragmatic.

All employees would be encouraged to take shares in the company.

The last point was important, for here was an enterprise that had just been announced and by 7 January had raised the initial £2 million to get it going. There was no guarantee at that time that the second tier – £16 million – would be raised; if it hadn't, the project would have floundered. But the founders were saying to their potential staff: 'Take a gamble as we have done but if the whole thing works, your shares could be worth real money in a few years' time.' For the first time in their careers journalists were being offered a stake in a business where they would be the chief asset. If it was a success the employees' stake could be worth £10 million when the company was floated in three or four years.

The message began to get home, and by the second week in January, many journalists had approached the founders seeking more information and expressing an interest in the project. At that stage, the founders believed that such was the importance of the journalists that they would account for just over half of the then total staff of 305. AWS said then: 'I have strong views on newspaper management. I don't want to make a paper where management cares nothing for the product and where journalists are unaware of the commercial consequences of what they do.' He spoke about his 1-2-3 principle for recruitment – that because the staff of a quality newspaper consists mainly of specialists, the three founders planned to identify the top three operators in each speciality 'from local government to golf' and then approach them. Salaries would be slightly above the going rates.

The first formal appointments, apart from the founders, were Douglas Long as Managing Director, and O'Neill as Advertisement and Marketing Director from 1 January. (O'Neill left his job on *TV Times* three days before he was to join the main board of Independent Television Publications). Linda Tanner, AWS' secretary of long-standing and a founder member, was appointed publicity officer.

A couple of weeks later, an event took place which completed Eddie Shah's one-man campaign to reform the state of British newspapers and which had a profound effect on the efforts to attract journalists to *The Independent*.

During the third week of January, Rupert Murdoch reached the end of the line in negotiations with the print unions at his four newspapers, *The Times*, *Sunday Times*, *The Sun* and *News of The World* over manning levels, new technology and the right to manage. The unions went on strike on 24 January and, over the next two days, the newspapers moved without them to a site that had taken years to build at Wapping. The unions' bluff had been called. Some 6,000 union members from secretaries to compositors, from van drivers to copy-takers, from press workers to librarians were told: either work at Wapping under new conditions of pay and employment or be sacked. All but a couple of handfuls held out.

It was a devastating move and Fleet Street's best-kept secret. For years it had been common knowledge that a new site was being prepared for *The Sun* and *News of the World* but no one believed that it would have the capacity to produce *The Times* and *Sunday Times* as well. The unions had always imagined that they could use those papers as a lever to obtain the best terms for a move to the new print works. Most union members believed, or were made to believe, that the newspapers could not be produced without their skill and craftsmanship, by non-union members.

The sudden move took all but a handful of journalists by surprise. They were shocked and deeply upset by what they saw as Murdoch's ruthless disregard for the livelihood of most of his employees. Some were only too glad to escape the tyranny of union monopoly and be in at the start of a revolution in national newspaper production. After a series of union meetings most of the journalists agreed reluctantly to go to Wapping. The management had offered them £2,000 increased salary (the management was reported later to have been willing to go as far as £6,000) and the assurance that their jobs would be safe. On Saturday, 25 January *The Sunday Times* and the *News of the World* were produced for the first time at Wapping by a handful of journalists, few of whom were members of the National Union of Journalists. The following day, Sunday, 26 January, the rest of the journalists began to arrive at Wapping to an entirely different way of working. A group of about 35 'refuseniks' refused to come and were promptly suspended without pay.

The journalists arrived to find that the move had been planned for many months. Externally the first impression was frightening – massive walls topped with 'razor wire' surrounded the huge complex. Giant gates sealed the sole main entrance. Floodlights pierced the New Year gloom and everywhere military-looking security men patrolled, speaking constantly into personal radios. Everyone had to stand in front of a camera to have a photograph taken for an identity card to be worn at all times and produced on request to anyone looking official.

Internally, the equipment was in place; there was an Atex VDT for most journalists, (unconnected) telephones were on allocated desks, there was a fully-functioning canteen. All journalists were given a sealed envelope on arrival which contained their secret password to enable them to have entry to the computer system (see chapter 7).

That weekend saw the start of some of the most violent picket line demonstrations ever seen in Britain. Journalists, print workers (not members of the NGA or SOGAT) and secretaries either drove through a gauntlet of hundreds, sometimes thousands, of taunting, abusive pickets or caught an 'armoured' coach to arrive at what soon became universally known as 'Fortress Wapping'. All members of staff who had come to Wapping were advised not to walk through the gates, such was the risk to life and limb. Ranks of policeman, many in riot gear, tried to keep the peace and allow the personnel coaches and the newspaper-carrying lorries to leave the complex or compound.

The traumatic and lasting effect the experience had on many journalists can scarcely be appreciated by anyone who was not there. Many felt intense sympathy for the sacked print workers – men and women they had been working next to only days before.

The Wapping dispute which was to drag on violently for many more months was both a blessing and nearly a blow for *The Independent*. David Porter at de Zoete and Bevan was worried that the huge cost saving generated by sacking all the print workers would spoil the attraction of *The Independent's* own low-cost base to potential investors. The era of post-Wapping newspaper economics had been born. Also the violence hardly gave the launch of a 'new-tech' newspaper a good public profile. In the event those fears proved groundless. The blessing lay in the desire by 90 per cent of journalists on *The Times* and 50 per cent on *The Sunday Times* to try to escape from Wapping and what they saw as the declining standards of the Murdoch papers as soon as possible.

In the weeks and months following the move to Wapping many dozens of applications were received by the founders from journalists there. For some the chance to flee Wapping was not the main reason, but the attraction of the new paper combined with the chance to leave the pickets and authoritarian atmosphere behind proved irresistible. For some the 'blacking' of Wapping journalists by the Labour Party and the union movement, proved too much. Among the first journalists to be appointed were, naturally enough, the heads of departments and sections – Nigel Lloyd, Production Editor (ex-*Observer*), David Brewerton, City Editor (ex-*Telegraph*), Sarah Hogg, Business and Finance Editor (ex-*Times*), Charles Burgess, Sports Editor (ex-*Guardian*), Tom Sutcliffe, Arts Editor (ex-BBC), Anthony Bevins, Political Editor (ex-*Times*).

The three-man team of Labour journalists on *The Times*, Don Macintyre, David Felton and Barrie Clement, who refused to go to Wapping, were picked up by AWS in one swoop. By the middle of April the three founders had seen dozens of applicants. All along they were careful to say that the second tier of finance had not been completed and that people should not irrevocably commit themselves to the new newspaper until that time. On 17 April the raising of the money was finalised and shortly afterwards AWS gave a party for all the journalists who had agreed to come. I left my job officially as Editor, Special Projects, on *The Times* at the end of May having spent many weeks from March onwards going in the morning or evening to City Road to help out. For me it was like a home from home with so many familiar faces from Wapping.

The list began to grow – David Hewson, Deputy Features Editor (ex-*Times*); Jonathan Fenby, Home Editor (ex-Reuters), Clare Dobie, financial writer (ex-*Times*). From *The Daily Telegraph*, Tom Kyte, Deputy City Editor and Tony Allen-Mills, Southern Africa Correspondent; from the *Sunday Telegraph*, Sebastian Faulks, Literary Editor; from *The Times*, poet and author, James Fenton, Far East Correspondent; from *The Guardian*, Maggie Brown, Media Editor.

Symonds tried to identify why so many had applied: 'We're not offering enormous salaries. In fact one or two people have taken a cut in salary to join us. We have a scale and stick to it. We pay market rates. We haven't bribed anyone to come.' He suggested in mid-May 1986 that the early appointments had had a snowball effect, that when potential staff had realised the quality of the people already taken on, they wanted to jump aboard themselves. Many journalists were surprised to discover that the planning that had gone into the entire operation had extended to the job applications. Journalists seeking specialist posts had to write out a paper describing how they would tackle the job and would then face an interview where their ideas would be discussed.

Glover was surprised by the number and enthusiasm of the applicants, saying that even supposedly cynical journalists had been attracted by such a project because of what it stood for.

An illustration of those independent principles which attracted a lot of attention among Fleet Street journalists was the decision to opt out of the Lobby briefing system. Under this practice, accredited political journalists would attend meetings called by the Prime Minister's Press Secretary to be given collective and non-attributable briefings about Government policies or action. It was the view of Anthony Bevins and AWS that the collective Lobby briefing tied journalists together in a band. Bevins: 'They know that if they take the easy way out, and report what Ingham [Bernard Ingham, then the Prime Minister's Press Secretary] tells them, they will not be vulnerable to the midnight phone call from newsdesks asking them to follow stories which have been reported faithfully by the opposition. By renouncing the Lobby system we believe that we will be forced to work that much harder, using our own sources and resources to do our job as journalists.' The move away from the Lobby made many journalists attentive because it attacked one of the basic methods and customs of political reporting.

Another, and it must be said, less popular decision was that of refusing to accept 'freebies' or free holidays, airline tickets or trips, be it from the Government, airlines or travel companies.

The appointments grew: Chris McKane, Deputy Home Editor (ex-*Times*); John Price, Assistant Home Editor (ex-*Times*); Harvey Morris, Assistant Foreign Editor (ex-Reuters); Nicholas Ashford, Deputy Foreign Editor (ex-*Times*); Oliver Gillie, Health Editor (ex-*Sunday Times*); Peter Wilby, Education Editor (ex-*Sunday Times*); Elkan Allan, TV and Listings Editor (ex-*Sunday Times*); John Bryant, Features Editor (ex-*Daily Mail* but who changed his mind and ended up going to *The Times* before launch). Departmental heads were getting their first taste of their budgets and finding that in many areas they were embarrassed for choice in terms of offering jobs. About the middle of May, *The Times* was putting on a brave face over the mass exodus from Wapping, saying that most people were leaving because of promotion, both in terms of more money and a title. Several *Times* journalists who had been approached by *The Independent* were offered huge salary rises to stay at Wapping, some did but many didn't.

Others who had resigned (most people were on four months' notice) were being told that, contrary to normal procedures, they would have to work out their entire notice period. It was known by then that *The Independent* was planning to run dummy issues for some time before launch and it made sound commercial sense to try to spoil that as much as possible. However, in the first week of June, about 20 journalists who had resigned from *The Times* and *Sunday Times* were told that they could leave immediately. Within a few days they did and arrived at *The Independent* earlier than planned.

By the end of June about 115 journalists had been hired – nearly one-third of them from Wapping. Although the three founders had come from *The Daily Telegraph*, at that stage only nine journalists had come from *The Daily Telegraph* and *Sunday Telegraph*. Five had come from the *Daily Mail*, four from *The Guardian*, four from the *Financial Times* and one from *Today*. Others had come from *The Economist*, the BBC, Reuters and the Press Association. The paper had received by then between 1,500 and 2,000 applications. AWS in June: 'I think in about 80 per cent to 85 per cent of cases we have got the person we were going for.'

At that time it had become apparent that earlier plans virtually to dispense with sub-editors would not work. The founders had originally imagined that the writers would be able to cut their own copy and even write their own headlines. This rapidly proved unworkable and a late drive went on to recruit sub-editors. Despite that, the newspaper remains very much a writer's publication. Sub-editors are given little freedom to re-write copy, especially articles from some of the 'star' foreign specialists. The number of journalists needed grew to 175. Although the majority of senior posts had gone to Fleet Street journalists, many others were to come from the provinces.

A small group of journalists came on the payroll on 1 July and the rest arrived in small numbers between then and launch. Some of the very first dummies were produced by about 10 people and the first printed dummies by about 110 journalists. In the end, 40 people in all joined from Wapping, providing a shared experience, relief at having escaped, and often a long-standing experience of working together.

In this chapter I have concentrated on the employment of journalists but it should be noted that during the same period intensive recruitment was going on in every department of the newspaper with many excellent advertising, marketing, circulation and production people being attracted to the new venture. At the end of November 1987, the total number of employees was 403. Of that total, there were 209 journalists and editorial support (including secretaries); 80 in advertising and marketing; 22 in circulation; 20 in production and operations; 41 in finance and administration; 6 executive directors; 21 departmental heads; 4 non-executive directors. Compared with the thousands who worked on other upmarket daily newspapers in the past, the number seemed ridiculously small.

King's Cross workmen taking a break during the clearing up operations
after the fire in November 1987. (Photo: Keith Dobney)

5: The Planning

Histories make men wise.

Francis Bacon (1561–1626)

Appearance

The appearance of a newspaper is something that most readers readily take for granted and seldom question. The design, typography and layout is there. It either works in their terms or they will switch to another newspaper. With the launch of *The Independent* as the first quality newspaper for 131 years, it is instructive and interesting to leaf through the dusty files of newspapers to see where layout and design began and how they have conditioned our thinking and acceptance of what we read today. Throughout the history of newspapers the progress of technology has dictated the appearance of the printed word and the final, and finite, control of the product.

The lessons of the past, consciously or unconsciously, determined the design decisions about *The Independent* as I shall demonstrate in subsequent chapters. Familiarity allied to subtle variation in the presentation of the written word ensures readership; experimentation rarely does. For example, why do we accept as normal eight-column pages or headlines in different type sizes?

The birth of the British newspaper can be traced to the publication of *The Oxford Gazette* on 16 November 1665. Why Oxford? The Great Plague of London had driven the Court northwards and a certain Joseph Williamson, the Under-Secretary of State for the Southern Department (in charge of Catholic affairs) was able to break the monopoly of news publication then controlled by Sir Roger L'Estrange in return for a pension of £100.

It was a significant breakthrough. From the start in the 1620s news pamphlets, *The Intelligencer*, *The Perfect Diurnall*, had been printed in book form. In 1643, the *Perfect Occurrences of Parliament* ran what we would now call summary points underneath its masthead in italic. These were possibly the first real headlines. The seeds of modern typography and newspaper design had been planted.

The Oxford Gazette abandoned the book format and picked up the style of the early Dutch corantos, the English pamphlets published in Holland in the early part of the century. It was a half-sheet which measured $11\frac{1}{4}$ inches (28cms) by $6\frac{3}{4}$ inches (16.8 cms). Each side, made up of two 17-pica columns separated by a vertical fine rule, was printed. The normal 12pt or pica text type size was reduced to bourgeois (9pt) thus allowing far more words to be printed. This switch heralded the start of the English typo-graphical movement.

The next significant step in typography took place when the first daily newspaper appeared, *The Daily Courant* on 11 March 1702. A few years earlier the press had become free when Parliament refused to renew the Restoration's Licensing Act and therefore removed all barriers to the production and growth of newspapers. *The Courant*, one side of a half-sheet, was published in Ludgate Hill, next to Fleet Street, by Edward Mallet. After nine issues it was taken over by Samuel Buckley, the first real newspaper pu-blisher, who also published and printed *The Spectator* from its start in 1711. *The Courant* expanded under Buckley, sometimes reaching as many as six pages.

Three-column make-up came in with the advent of *The Daily Journal* in 1720 and *The Daily Advertiser* in 1730. The title was a line in roman upper and lower case across the page. Blackletter for main titles and white-lined black letter came much later. About 1770, the three-column page gave way in some instances to the four-column page which was to remain the standard width for many years. It was limited by the size of the wooden hand-press which could print two folio pages in one go. The column width varied from 14 to 16 picas. It is worth noting how long it took to take proofs or pulls of the pages – 200 an hour was an acceptable target from one wooden press. Later duplicate, triplicate and quadruplicate setting was necessary to increase circulation. Already newspaper expansion and growth was being restricted by old technology.

By the 1780s the format of the daily newspapers on sale in London had been fixed with four four-column pages with adver-tisements big and small adorning the whole of the front page. Of crucial importance in the development of newspapers was the birth of *The Daily Universal Register* on 1 January 1785. Three years later it was renamed *The Times*. Advertisements were to remain on its front page until 3 May 1966. The original reason for their appearance on the front page was the importance placed in London at that time on the theatrical announcements or 'bills'. Advertising was also seen by some newspaper publishers as more important to their readers than the news, which was often relegated to a back or inside page.

Typography continued to develop with white-lined blackletter, typefaces especially designed for newspapers and leading or spacing between paragraphs. A pioneer in the latter respect was publisher John Bell who ran *The World* (1787) and *The Oracle* (1789). Richard Austin, a punch-cutter at his British Letter Foundry, produced the first modern British typeface, later known as Bell Roman. As Allen Hutt says in his remarkable book, *The Changing Newspaper* (Gordon Fraser, London, 1973), the new typeface was to give 'newspaper text its own distinctive flavour instead of being a narrow-measure version of book typography using the familiar classic typefaces of the book printer.'

The Times followed on in November 1799 with a typeface from the foundry of Mrs Elizabeth Caslon. The Caslon typeface, to be used by so many newspapers over the centuries, was a direct descendant of the Bodoni typeface, latterly identified with *The Daily Telegraph*. Both the Bell roman and the Caslon had achieved a degree of condensing the characters to save space, an essential criterion given the stamp duty then payable on newspapers.

The typographical changes that took place in the late 1700s were to remain in place with minor adjustments until the 1920s. However, developments in printing technology would soon play a great part in the evolution of modern newspaper design. The advent of the iron press enabled *The Times* in 1811 to switch over to a five-column page but increasing pressure from taxes resulted in advertising and news being crammed in with little or no regard for art or symmetry.

As Hutt said: 'Any attempts at display, any exploitation of typographic art, vanished from *The Times* just as, under its first outstanding publisher, John Walter II, and its first independent editor, Thomas Barnes (The Thunderer), it began to forge ahead to its extraordinary position of journalistic and political near-monopoly.' In 1817, when Barnes was named editor, *The Times* was able to cope with a circulation of 7,000 a day, thanks to the introduction of the first power-driven printing machines in Printing House Square in November 1814. These Koenig and Bauer cylinder machines increased the output of the old hand press five-fold.

The Times adopted a six-column make-up in 1825 and its paging increased to eight pages in 1833. Further advances were afoot with the invention of the forerunner of the modern rotary press in the mid-1840s. The problem until then had been how the circulation of a newspaper could be allowed to increase given the restrictions imposed by the presses. The limits of production through the use of a flat-bed cylinder machine where the impression was taken by a revolving cylinder from a reciprocating forme on the bed of the machine had long been reached.

The solution, arrived at independently by Augustus Applegath in London and Hoe in New York, was to turn the printing surface into a rotating cylinder. By 1860, the new generation of presses were installed in London at *The Daily Telegraph*, the *Standard*, *The Daily News* and *The Times*. *The Telegraph* claimed to run its new presses at 18,000 copies an hour and *The Times* at 13,000. Circulation increases stemming from the interest in the Crimean War (1854–56) could be coped with. Again new technology proved the key to expansion. Printing developments continued apace but newspapers were still squeezed by the heavy Stamp Acts and packed in their material.

To quote Stanley Morison, the great typographer, in his book *Printing The Times*: 'While the news trade expanded economically as the handmaid and sometimes slave of commercial publicity, the newspapers fell backward as pieces of typography and their staffs as skilled designers of print.' Despite the introduction of curved stereoplates which would enable the type to be expanded across more than one column, an innate conservatism in design had set in. The printers made up the pages in the best way they could think of to squeeze in all the advertisements they had received. Verticality was the order of the day and for years into the future. The one advance in *The Times* was the increasing use of 'titlings' or capital headings in 14pt type size followed by 10pt type size above the news stories. This was not to last. By 1860, *The Times* had settled on a 10pt light single-column titling that was to remain virtually unchanged for 50 years. Newspaper design stayed in the doldrums. *The Times* was the role model for the morning newspapers and newspapers were a profitable business and not an art form. The single-column titlings were soon adopted by newspapers up and down Britain.

Shortly before and after the turn of the century, trends in newspaper presentation in America and the Continent began to spread across to Britain. In the late 1890s, after Alfred Harmsworth took over the *Evening News*, headlines were developed and the first multi-column banner appeared in 1895 in it. Nevertheless, it was not until 1901 that any morning newspaper used a double-column headline. Photographs were becoming increasingly popular replacing the old woodcuts still being used by some newspapers.

The Star followed transatlantic custom and introduced stacking American-type headlines in 1888. The Linotype machine was introduced in 1886 but was not equipped to set type at more than 14pt. Despite the strict conservatism in typography, *The Times* began to introduce double- or even triple-deck headlines. The layout, as always, remained vertical.

The First World War had a dramatic effect on the fortunes of newspapers. Even *The Times*, for a few exceptional Sundays, had news on its front page. It searched through its advertising cases for different typefaces. A mixture of Caslon, Bodoni, Cheltenham and Venetian appeared. Half-tone blocks were brought in for the first time in 1914. It still retained its six column measure, although the other London daily newspapers had switched over to seven. But these revolutionary moves again proved too much and the use of small news-titlings was to continue until 1932. In 1921 *The Times* finally changed over to seven columns of a 14pica width. By the end of 1923, *The Times* began to alternate its headings with light and heavy fonts (variations in the typeface). Also by then the essential regular placing of features had been established.

The great typographical revolution, reversing the text style of the previous 130 years, was to come from Stanley Morison, the inspiration for a new generation of typographers. In 1929 he was appointed to *The Times* as their typographical adviser and given the gargantuan task of designing a new typeface for the newspaper. His definition of what that new typeface should be is a model of sense and sensibility. He said it should be 'worthy of *The Times* — masculine, English, direct, simple, not more novel than it behoveth to be novel . . . and absolutely free from faddishness and frivolity.'

Morison's sketches were redrawn by Victor Lardent and later cut by the Monotype Corporation. Times New Roman first appeared in the newspaper on 3 October 1932 in sizes ranging from $5\frac{1}{2}$ pt to 9pt. Six new designs of headlines in the same face appeared – in a range that ran from 7pt to 48pt. Morison's rationale was as follows '. . . thus the whole range . . . bears a family likeness which guarantees harmony but, owing to the variation in width and weight, avoids monotony.' Perhaps. The title on the front page was also changed after much argument from Gothic to roman caps. However the tombstone layout remained and was to remain for many more years.

His great new typeface was used exclusively by *The Times* for one year and then released for general use. It became and is still the most widely-used and admired twentieth-century general text type and a variation of it is used on *The Independent* under the name of Dutch.

Throughout the twentieth century until the sixties when other publications were changing traditional designs and when magazines such as *Picture Post* and *Life* were showing what could be done with decent photographs, *The Times* retained its reputation for lofty indifference to changing trends in visual communication.

It was almost as though the newspaper was so secure in its reputation for news-reporting and analysis and comment in its once-thundering leader columns that it felt it was unnecessary to advertise its daily wares in such an obvious way as on the front page. How vulgar that would be. And how wrong it would be to acknowledge the modern world of visual display. Politicians perhaps, priests, professors and lawyers certainly would think it a terrible exercise in self-display. It would be an unnecessary flaunting of journalistic excellence that had been taken for granted for so many years.

And yet perhaps they were right. Should not a newspaper of serious intent and scholarship reflect those qualities in its appearance? It had no need, until the economic realities of the 1960s, to change the wrapping-paper to attract new customers. Its readership was catholic in taste, reactionary in style. Modernism in art, music and literature had to be recognised in a spirit of liberal tolerance but that did not mean the gentlemen journalists of *The Times* had to reflect those changes in any way in their newspaper.

In layout terms, Morison had set the seal in 1932 along with his new typography: 'If ever *The Times* accepts double-column headings, it will not be because they are necessary but because a generation of readers has been habituated to them by reading journals less scrupulously conducted.' He was, or course, referring to the tabloid press which had been experimenting with double-column headlines since the turn of the century. The first double column appeared that year on 2 December but only one per page at most was permissible.

This passive view of layout was symptomatic of a more general feeling of effortless superiority that had existed on *The Times* throughout most of its history. The sobriety of approach and a lack of interest in any design beyond the merely functional or informative was continued in the size and strength of headlines and photographs. Everything was calm and austere. The headline writers reflected the sober production of the writers; any attempt at levity or appeal through bold headline presentation or words was frowned on.

Looking back over the files of *The Times* with the hindsight of the last 20 years when newspaper design has become far more of an accepted art and skill, the impression one receives is that for years nothing was allowed to prevent the reader reaching the text of the articles as soon as possible – a fine principle if the words are well-written. Perhaps it did not occur to the editors that dull but worthy stories could be made attractive and enlivened by more exciting layout, presentation and witty headline writing. For years articles were even unsigned, all part and parcel of the denial of personality; Sir William Haley, editor of *The Times* from 1952–1966, said : 'Signed writing invites exhibitionism.' And exhibitionism was equated with a regrettable display of passion and creativity.

Photographs were used in much the same way on the quality newspapers. They were seen as an occasional adornment to capture a suitably dramatic set-piece of history. Admittedly Lord North-cliffe, then owner of *The Times*, asked for a daily picture page in 1922. The newspaper's first art editor, who also served as picture editor for 35 years, Ulric Van den Bogaerde, father of actor and writer Dirk Bogarde, readily complied and gave a new strength to pictures on pages. Despite that, pictures were still frowned upon by most of the writers. It is worth noting that Bogaerde in a true pioneering way was also the first photographer to capture scenes from theatre and dance using natural light, thus dispensing with the previous reliance on hard artificial light and posed pictures.

The Times was to maintain its position both in the newspaper market and in terms of layout with little change between 1932 and 1966. Then, shortly before the take-over by the Thomson Organisation, news arrived on the front page. Sir William Haley acknowledged the insularity of his newspaper: 'The days when *The Times* could be satisfied with addressing a small national elite are gone.' More radical changes were to follow; a new masthead, or title-piece, a change, finally, to an eight-column measure (April 1967) and further changes in headline typography. The pattern of what exists today was forming. The major layout revolution of that period came in September 1970 when *The Times* introduced what was to become known as modular make-up. The entire emphasis was on horizontal presentation and the use of multi-line headlines in smaller than usual point sizes. It is interesting to note here that *The Times* was able by this step to remove, almost entirely, 'fillers' (one or two paragraph stories used to fill in gaps where stories fell short) from its front page.

Despite the attractiveness of Morison's original Times New Roman, the problems of setting its delicate outlines also caused a new typeface, Times Europa, to be introduced on 9 October 1972. The troubles and effects of trying to introduce new technology at Grays Inn Road and the move to Wapping have been well-documented elsewhere. However, in terms of this book, the necessity to print at Wapping caused a further blow to the years of quiet and patient evolution of the newspaper when the width of *The Times* had to be reduced to twice the size of its tabloid stable-mate, *The Sun*, to enable it to be printed on the same presses. Morison must have turned in his grave.

I have necessarily concentrated on the evolution of *The Times* since it was for so long the role model for serious newspapers in content, style and presentation. It is worth taking a brief look at the other newspapers at the quality side of the market where *The Independent* was subsequently to end up.

The Daily Telegraph, while not quite reaching the monastic severity of *The Times*, displayed until very recently no signs of regard for the visual appeal of its forbidding columns. Design, again took a backward step. A newspaper was to be read for its content on a regular basis. It was a daily constitutional. Perhaps at times the track was a little muddy but it was something its readers could feel thoroughly at home with. A trusted and comfortable suit handed down from an uncle which could be worn by successive generations and show few signs of wear and tear.

An overall look for the newspaper had evolved without many radical changes for years. Its essential problem in design terms was its template approach. Its rigidity in make-up stifled its reaction to news events. As Harold Evans says in his book, *Newspaper Design* (Heinemann, London, 1973): 'The layout as well as the format is fixed, so as to combine, oddly enough, a functionally designed format and a non-functional layout. The static layout fixes a pattern of headlines, text and picture positions and pours the news into moulds every day.'

This static layout is exemplified in the regular use of a double- or three-column lead headline on the left-hand side of the front page, a regularly-sized three column picture next to that and a second story, in terms of importance, in columns 7 and 8. The pattern is repeated on inside pages. Typographically the paper has been more exciting. Up to the 1960s *The Telegraph* had the traditional all-capitals stacked or decker headlines in Century. Ten years later an overall style using a Bodoni typeface had been adopted, providing a clean, if perhaps, boring consistency.

Under the more recent editorship of Max Hastings, *The Telegraph* has become slightly more adventurous, but a reader returning to civilisation and his favoured newspaper after 20 years on a desert island would hardly be shocked or attracted by the change.

The Guardian followed most of the typographical advancements of its rivals but generally produced a more balanced layout on its news pages. While not as static as *The Telegraph*, its pages provided little encouragement for the reader with the use of short headlines both in numbers of words and number of decks or lines. From the late 1960s until recently it has produced exemplary modular layout on its feature pages with unassuming yet effective use of headline weights and typography. On 12 February 1988, *The Guardian* appeared with a radical redesign. Using Helvetica and Garamond typefaces, the entire paper was redesigned providing a so-called 'continental' appearance and magazine look. It was a bold move and may appeal to a new, younger and more design-conscious generation of newspaper readers.

Then, of course, there is the *Financial Times*, a model of design absolutism. Its structure is unique; its appearance distinctive and daunting. Unlike other newspapers, it is the only indispensable one for a large group of professional people around the world. The key to its success is information allied to informed comment. Its only distinguishing visual characteristic, apart from endless columns of statistical information, is its pink colour. Perhaps its appeal lies in its very lack of visible design on the majority of its pages.

How then should *The Independent* look? It was a problem that perhaps caused more anxiety and contradiction than any other. The decisions about financing, production, technology and staff were taken on a far more rational basis. How can a newspaper aiming at the well-established quality market take on an appearance that does not mirror existing newspapers but does not alienate potential readers through too radical a design? How can it provide something that is at once eye-catching and sympathetic to the use of long and well-informed articles?

Should it even place much reliance on design or simply aim for a bland and unassuming appearance that allows the writing to stand by itself? Of course it is far too late, and rightly so, to return to the days when the design of quality newspapers was the least factor to be considered in the daily production process. As we have seen above, the tide turned during the 1960s, 1970s and 1980s when quality newspapers began to produce well-designed pages with decent pictures that complemented the writing.

Harold Evans, editor of *The Sunday Times* from 1967 to 1981, editor of *The Times* from 1981 to 1982, and his design editor, Edwin Taylor, helped to inspire a new generation of sub-editors, layout artists, picture editors and design editors who realised that the time when the basic page design followed a regular template day in day out until the big disaster story broke was past. Gone too was the practice of creating a page and leaving a hole for a picture often without reading the articles or seeing the actual photograph that was to be used on it.

He inspired journalists to see that a quality newspaper need not only be informative and worthy, it could also be attractive and appealing at the same time. There were the detractors who claimed that he was bringing serious journalism down to the level of the tabloids. Far from it, he was bringing a new style and form of presentation to broadsheet journalism. He was bold enough to suggest that a really excellent sports picture could be worth a thousand words. What he did was to codify what had been thought of by many other journalists and practised in a haphazard way around the world. His philosophy over the use of pictures contained little that had not been tried at one stage or another. Newspaper history abounds with examples of the brilliant use of photographs; he merely explained why and how they should be used, to a large and receptive audience lurking in the art departments of Fleet Street.

I have tried to demonstrate in this chapter how the design and layout of newspapers had come about and what lessons from that growth could be applied to *The Independent*. The serious newspapers had formed a style of presentation that for many years owed more to the ability of their printers to cram in as much type as possible and the ability of their primitive presses to cope with increased volume than to any overall and finite design. Old technology and editorial conservatism had conditioned the market acceptability of the serious newspapers. Years of consistency had established the School of the Quality Newspapers. A regular reader could spot them from afar and not get confused by the tabloid intruders. Art and craft had mainly been devoted to typography.

It was in this environment that the appearance of *The Independent* would develop in the months before launch. It could not look like a tabloid but equally it could not resemble too closely its putative rivals, *The Times*, *The Telegraph*, *The Guardian* and the *Financial Times*.

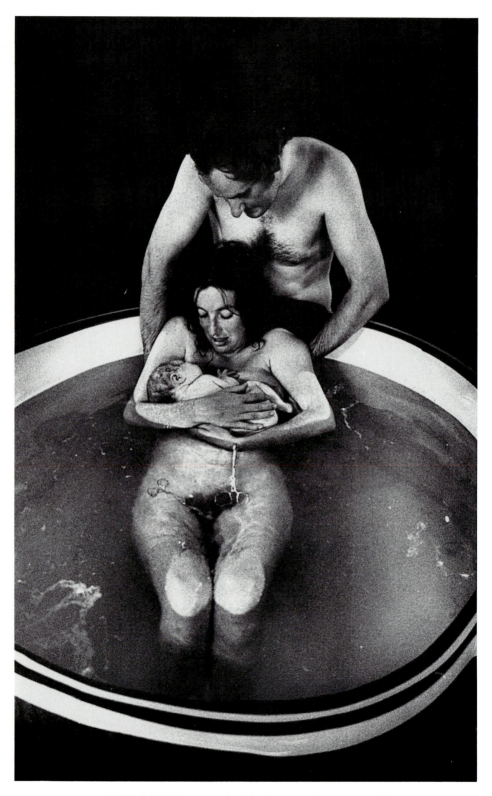

'Natural Childbirth' photographed in August 1987 by David Rose.

6: The Planning

*A newspaper is a vehicle for transmitting
news and ideas. The design is an integral
part of that process. We begin with a
blank sheet of newsprint and a mosaic of
ideas we want to communicate and it is the
function of newspaper design to present that
mosaic in an organised and comprehensible way.*

Harold Evans (1928–)

Design

AWS has always freely admitted that he had had no real experience
or knowledge of design before work began on *The Independent*.
Equally he has always told me that he knows what he does not like
when he sees it. He and his other co-founders had looked at both
British and foreign newspapers, especially the quality newspapers
in France, America and Spain and had some idea of how *The
Independent* should look.

He was to say later that it was the hardest thing he had to do. He
compared it to being driven in a car on an icy road – he had to rely
on the people handling it and had to use his skill in handling people
to control them and keep the car on the road. He was forced to
drive the car from the back seat when it came to design.

What size?

Some decisions do not, at first, seem to merit serious or detailed
analysis. It becomes rapidly obvious that a serious newspaper
should have a broadsheet shape. It is a custom and practice that
would be immensely difficult to break. Why can one be so certain?

British newspaper readers equate tabloid-size newspapers with
tabloid-quality journalism. This is unfair to the many good
examples of journalism that appear in British tabloid newspapers
every day but it is a widely-held view. Tabloids should be treated
more as a size of newspapers rather than a standard of merit. In
conventional printing terms a tabloid can vary in size – it depends
on the dimensions of the rotary cylinder of the press it is being
printed on. A broadsheet newspaper is as deep as the circum-
ference of a rotary plate cylinder. A tabloid on the same press is half
that size. The advantages of web-offset production are only now
being explored on national newspapers, including *The Independent*. Traditionally a broadsheet varies in size from about 21 inches
(533mm) to 26 inches (660mm). There are some quirks thrown up

by unusual rotary sizes. For example, *Le Monde*, the Paris-based upmarket quality daily, is a large tabloid at $13\frac{1}{4}$ inches (337mm) by $19\frac{1}{2}$ inches (495mm).

In any discussion about the shape of a new newspaper the practical advantages of tabloids should be considered. They are a convenient size to buy, read, fold, hold and carry. It is much easier to organise and place advertising and editorial on a tabloid. For example a favourite size of advertisement is 38cms (15.2 inches) by 6 broadsheet columns; on a broadsheet an advertisement that size dominates the page causing immense problems for the designer; on a tabloid it is a full page. It is also much easier to design and make-up a tabloid page.

The broadsheet has its own advantages apart from its association with serious journalism. A broadsheet format can enable the editor to carry longer stories and a bigger round-up of stories on the same subject on one page without the necessity to carry them over to a following page. It enables the designer to use much bigger pictures and graphics than on a tabloid. That in turn enables the designer to produce far more attractive fashion or sports pages, for example, which have come to rely on strong visual characteristics. In news terms, a well-designed broadsheet front page has massive advantages over a tabloid.

Not the least consideration in any debate about the relative merits of tabloid versus broadsheet must be cost, time and wastage. Far more newsprint is used every time a broadsheet page is folded in two to become a tabloid; having twice as many pages, tabloids cost more in time and money on presses, both old and new, in plate- or negative-making.

With all those factors in mind *The Independent* was destined to be a broadsheet. There was debate at some stage during early 1986 about the attractions of *Le Monde*. It has been said that it does not bother with such vulgarities as design. On first glance, of course it is austere and sterile; there are no half-tone pictures to break the greyness, no sudden visual brush strokes of daring layout to attract the eye. Harold Evans on *Le Monde*: 'The renunciation of photographs, the sizing of headlines and the whole arrangement of the paper are all in themselves attempts to accommodate, in logical design, the editorial philosophy of being a paper of serious news and interpretation rather than a paper of 'spot' news, surprise and entertainment.'

In previous chapters we have examined the philosophy behind *The Independent* and its recruitment of staff. The designers and the design were to prove the most difficult. There was no-one available who had designed a new serious upmarket national newspaper in Britain – there had not been a new one for 131 years.

The designers:

Stephen Hitchins, the first designer to work on *The Independent*, was introduced by Linda Tanner to AWS who wanted someone to produce new designs for the City pages of *The Telegraph* early in

1985. In fact the contract went to David Hillman of Pentagram although his designs were not taken up. But when AWS was looking for a designer again he approached Hitchins in October 1985. Saatchi and Saatchi had already endorsed the project and it was time to try to put some of their findings and the editorial wishes of the founders into a practical shape and form to use in market research. As the founders were still working at *The Telegraph*, Hitchins had to do all his initial work in secret. He and his team at Archigrafia presented various ideas for mastheads and the layout of pages. These presentations were usually carried out in his offices in the mornings or at AWS's home in the late evening or at weekends. The concept of large folios, page titles, thin and thick rules, general layout considerations and the chiselled masthead were almost cemented before Christmas 1985.

Hitchins and his team stopped work for the Christmas holidays and then the *Financial Times* broke the story on 27 December. On New Year's Eve, the founders spent the last few hours on *The Telegraph's* payroll working in Hitchins' office. Hitchins was still devising new mastheads in a variety of typefaces and different titles (see chapter 1).

Work continued on producing printed dummies. Hitchins was aware that the newspaper would be produced on 'state of the art' technology. Atex and Xenotron page-layout equipment was by then already pencilled in. He tried to reflect the technological advantages in his dummies which demonstrate a cleanness that has carried through right to launch.

Hitchins remembers that at the time, from the information received from potential printers, it was thought that it would only be feasible for the new newspaper to be produced in two sections. He placed the information and What's On guide on the back of the first section. The front of the second section was Business News with Sport at the back, a formula very like *The Times* today. Everyone was happier when, before long, the paper became integrated.

At the time the founders were hoping to use colour in a way that had never been possible before on a British national daily. Problems arose because of the incompatibility of the regional print plants that were going to produce the newspaper. Some could produce it on one page, others on different pages. It was a problem that would remain with the newspaper long after launch. Hitchins: ' I do not think that the client had ever realised that so little colour would be available, that spot colour would not be available throughout, and that total compatibility would severely limit our choice of just where colour could fall.'

Hitchins and his team were by then working very much to the ground rules laid down by the founders. Some of them were to remain in operation to the present day:

1) A broadsheet format.

2) No turning stories from the front page.

3) Articles would be longer than normal in other newspapers.

Overleaf, two early dummies produced by Stephen Hitchins in January 1986.

THE INDEPENDENT

No 1
MONDAY OCTOBER 6 1986
25p

Special Report
Crisis in France

News Digest

King apologises for Ulster gaffe

A day-long bid by King, Northern Ireland Secretary, expressed regret on a ministerial statement for having suggested that Sir Edward, in his call for an independent Scotland, in a united Ireland. Page 2 and 5

Jaruzelski visit shocks France

The first visit by the Polish leader, General Jaruzelski, to a western head of Government has led to the impression of normal row caused consternation in France. President Mitterand attacked by the special editorial, The Elysee Palace. by the back door. Page 2 and 6

Mrs Jarrett's death accidental

Mrs Cynthia Jarrett's death, which sparked riots, has been accidental, an inquiry by Brent Council social services committee to staff for gross misconduct. This follows the inquiry into the death of a four-old. Rosemary the school, whose stepfather has been manslaughter. The document was found. Watkins, responsible for running Watkins. Broadwater is supervisor over the proceedings of officer Tom Bryant Social News, a supervisor who has completed appeared for police Page 2 and 4

Goal for animal rights activists

Seven animal rights activists were jailed for their Animal Rights Trade on Saturday when leaders attacked in connection with charges. Thirteen faced charges for their trials is the most serious. Page 2 and 5

NUM climbdown on productivity

The officers of the National Power of Mineworkers may today made to impose last week over their bonus productivity payments. Arthur Scargill's leaders have rejected again a climb-down. Page 2 and 3

Britain to leave UNESCO

Britain is withdrawal from UNESCO, the United Nations Educational, Scientific and Cultural Organisation is expected to be announced today. Page 2 and 3

Joe Kennedy stands for Congress

Joseph Kennedy, the eldest son of the murdered Senator Robert Kennedy and nephew of President John Kennedy, is on cue for office. He is candidate for a Boston congressional district. Page 2 and 4

Bruno floors American

Frank Bruno, the European heavyweight champion from Wandsworth, knocked out Larry Frazer of the United States in the second round of a fight at the Royal Albert Hall in London Page 3 to 5

MP's favour rail channel

The Commons transport committee is expected to support a twin-rail tunnel link between Britain and France Page 3 to 1

Business Digest

STOCK MARKET		THE POUND	
FT 30 Share		US dollar	
1299.4 (+1.9)		1.4585 (+0.0045)	
FT-SE 100		W German mark	
1566.1 (−3.0)		3.2678 (−0.0095)	
USM (Datastream)		Trade-weighted	
115.45 (unch)		73.4 (+0.1)	

Murdoch's UK profits soar 85 pc to £34.5m

Brent Council social services committee last night sacked three staff for gross misconduct. This follows the inquiry into the death of a four-old Jasmine Beckford, whose stepfather has been jailed for her manslaughter. The dismissed social workers are Maureen Oct., as an administ. an inquiry into its disclosure, with London detailed yesterday. The Brent heads, and for London's and a vindication of their complaint against the police Page 2 and 4

PR firm in Gulliver row

The first visit by the Polish leader General Jaruzelski, to a western head of Government has led to consternation in France. President Mitterand attacked by the special editorial, The Elysee Palace by the back door. Page 2 and 6

Reagan names new adviser

President Reagan announced the resignation of Robert McFarlane as US National Security adviser and named as such a result of a personality clash within the White House. Page 4 and 5

Plessey rejects GEC

Plessey has rejected its £1.2 billion bid approach made by its General Electric company and registered with a proposal to buy out such a interest in the system 9 digital telephone exchanges Page 4 to 1

Scotland reaches soccer finals

Scotland drew 0-0 with Australia in Melbourne to reach the 1986 World Cup soccer finals due to be played in Mexico next year Page 24 and 5

Downing Street celebration

The Queen and the Duke of Edinburgh joined Mrs Thatcher and five former prime ministers for dinner at No 10 last week that have elapsed since the building first became prime minister's official residence.

MP's favour rail channel

The Commons transport committee is expected to support a twin-rail tunnel link between Britain and France Page 3 to 1

Low pay equals low interest rates

Mr Lawson, chancellor of the Exchequer told the National Economic Development Council that cheaper mortgages and moderate wage increases then less interest rates would be more likely. Page 1 and 5

Contents

Weather

London, SE, central S, E England, East Anglia, Midlands: Sunny intervals, scattered showers, perhaps thundery, becoming fewer, wind light becoming moderate. Max 16C (61F).

Channel Islands, SW, central S, W England: Sunny periods, scattered showers, wind light to moderate. Max 16C (61F).

NW England, Borders, Edinburgh, Dundee, Aberdeen, Glasgow, central Highlands, Moray Firth, NE Scotland: Sunny intervals, showers, wind moderate. Max 14C.

Outlook for tomorrow and Wednesday: mainly dry in the south, rather cloudy with some rain in the north later, becoming milder.

Sellafield now the 'World's dirtiest plant'

BY QUENTIN FAY IN BRUSSELS

An international scientific study has concluded that a surgical operation regularly performed in Britain is useless.

The operation, extracranial-intracranial arterial by-pass, is estimated to reduce the incidence of stroke, the third largest cause of death and disability in the West.

The results of the study, which involved seven years and a four-year follow-up in 14 surgical centres, found no benefit to patients in 14 countries. The conclusion is an option for treating these patients.

In the study, 700 patients who had recently recovered from a stroke underwent the surgery, while 700 others received conventional medical treatment.

Eventually, rates of those who did not recover had a single stroke within the next five years, compared with 18 per cent of the medical cases.

Eleven per cent of the surgical patients suffered stroke or major strokes, compared with 10 per cent of the others.

Surgeons have resorted to the operation since its introduction 14 years ago in the belief that it connected patients who had suffered a minor stroke and made a good recovery.

It has been concluded and argued widely that the re-establishment of general disease within the skull is an inevitable progress at the base of the brain.

The operation calls for considerable expertise and training in microvascular techniques. It is relatively safe, although costly in terms of surgical time. About 200 such by-passes are performed in Britain each year.

One of its leading practitioners, Professor Roger Greenhalgh, professor of surgery at a busy London hospital, said: "I will not abandon the operation. But I believe the study was used to have even more rigorous selection of patients than at present they have, or at present.

"I have been performing this operation for about eight years on patients who have been selected to receive it."

"The study, in very unpretentious, but it does show that some patients will have benefited. It is terribly important that we can identify those to whom the operation will be of no benefit, so that we can save them the ordeal of unnecessary surgery."

The last thing we must do is alarm patients. I believe this surgery is of value to those who have been most carefully selected to receive it."

Dr John Wade, a senior registrar in neurology at the National Hospital for Nervous Diseases in London, took part in the study. He said: "I believe the results emphasise the need for adequate trials when new surgical or medical treatments are introduced."

"If the risk of recurrence of stroke is relatively small even when nothing is done at all, the doctor may incorrectly attribute his patient's wellbeing to the surgery rather than the natural history of the untreated condition."

Professor Greenhalgh and colleagues are keen to devote more time to investigating methods of screening against stroke. "We must concentrate on finding effective ways to detect those people who are at great risk, and take preventative action," he said.

An editorial in the current issue of The Lancet praises the study which it describes as "a landmark trial in the assessment of any surgical procedure, and certainly in the surgical prevention of stroke."

The study cost £9 million (about £6.2 million). The Lancet says: "The cost was high but it will be repaid many times over if we accept the results and divert health care resources into things that do have an impact on reducing the incidence of stroke."

Source: The New England Journal of Medicine, November 1

Deadline threat to BA sale

BY RUPERT CORN

Some doctors are arguing that the situation has been made worse by cuts in the number of acute beds in and around London as money is transferred out of the four Thames regions.

Sixteen hospitals in the North-West Thames region, including inner London teaching hospitals, have been put on "red alert" by London's emergency Bed Service for the first time since the 1973 influenza epidemic, closing to all but emergency cases.

In the South East Thames region, out to Bexley and in Greater London and others in the Home Counties have halted non-urgent admissions to have closed to all except emergency cases as the effects of the cold spell on hospital admissions is felt.

In some cases for short periods hospitals have even had to close to emergency admissions.

The closures come as the numbers of elderly patients needing admission with bronchitis, pneumonia and hypothermia rose steeply during the recent cold spell and as beds became blocked by elderly patients who cannot safely be sent home quickly.

Cut in base rates expected

The Government aims to hit the pockets of criminals and improve compensation for victims in proposals published yesterday for its final law and order legislation before the general election.

The White Paper, one of the most wide-ranging series proposals on the criminal justice system since Mrs Thatcher came to power, covers increases in maximum sentences, faster extradition arrangements, measures to aid the prosecution of fraud and options for jury reform.

The Government is determined that crime must not pay and intends to put greater

More victims are expected to benefit from the Criminal Injuries Compensation Scheme, which is to be put on a statutory basis. That will give eligible applicants a definite right to receive compensation.

The Bill, also to be introduced in the next session of Parliament, is expected to give new powers to set criminals profits. Powers of courts in order to track the proceeds of property used in connection with crime would be strengthened.

Mr Douglas Hurd, the Home Secretary, said yesterday that measures to be brought forward in the Bill

Rex East "red alert"

externed with safeguards.

Bills further strengthening the Government's priorities, Mr Hurd said.

But Mr Gerald Kaufman, Shadow Home Secretary, denounced the White Paper as "a new patches of whitewash on a disgraceful Government record on crime". It was a classic example of closing the stable door after the horse had bolted.

"It basically has to do with what we do with criminals after they are caught. But 85 per cent of criminals are not caught — a much higher percentage of criminals getting away with their crimes than when this Government came into office."

Ministers rule over Vickers bid

BY DAVID LAW

In banking parlours, insurance offices and other financial intermediaries, there is a nagging fear. Is the Chancellor, strapped for Budget cash because of tumbling oil prices, about to introduce a new tax on financial services?

Rumours of a financial services tax appear before every Budget. This year they have been stronger, for two main reasons.

The first is that the banks appear to be doing very well. Yesterday, Barclays announced a 1985 profit of £634 million, 37 per cent up on the previous year.

Barclays was the last of the big clearers to report. All four have notched up a substantial profits improvement.

The strong profits performance of the banks and the fact that politicians, perhaps rightly, see the banks as widely regarded as a windfall profits tax on the banks. The tax raised £355 million in the 1981-82 financial year.

There are, however, good reasons for thinking that, if a new tax is introduced, it will not be in this form. In 1981 it could be argued that the banks had benefited at the expense of other sectors, notably manufacturing, from the Government's high interest rate strategy.

Although rates of interest have been high since the January 1985 profit of £634 and real rates even higher than in 1986, it is more difficult to make the case that the banks have benefited while other sectors have suffered. In addition, in 1981, monsters, excluding the present Chancellor, committed themselves to not reintroducing such a tax.

Mr Nigel Lawson, as Finan-

Defeat on finance bill

BY RAYMOND HUGH COURTS CORRESPONDENT

A High Court judge yesterday dismissed an attempt by Argyll Group to block Guinness's real £2.4 billion takeover bid for Distillers.

Argyll had asked for an order declaring illegal a decision by the Monopolies and Mergers Commission to lay aside its inquiry into the Guinness bid.

Mr Justice Macpherson said that had the Argyll case succeeded it would have put Guinness's bid, which has the backing of the Distillers directors, into "temporary cold storage", giving Argyll a clear field.

Argyll lawyers said after wards that they would appeal. £1 million but for accounting changes made because of altered circumstances.

Thatcher and Tebbit exclude Cabinet from manifesto

BY OUR FOREIGN AND FINANCIAL STAFF

Nearly everything succeeds most, from trading to shopping if the prospect for Britain in 1986 are depicted today by the Prime Minister and Mr Tebbit as the next four year messages.

Without Mrs Margaret Thatcher makes that Britain is "prospering hard" and has worked its way back to the top of the economic league table. The Labour leader predicts the country is to go further and off to take off of black and brown climate soar 35 per cent in the next four years.

The Prime Minister, attacking politicians who say success is leading to greater the successes and talks Britain down, says: "There are back those companies, management and workforce who are breaking all export records. Let us look closer trade unionists who, instead of striking and bringing their company to a standstill, were so busy at work. Let us look younger workers who have the get up and go and get to start up business of own. Let us look back Britain and take pride in our own."

Developers have been saying the Mr Robert James, improving

that, ever before and paying its way in the world. She speaks of "a resurgence of enterprise" thousands of extra firms and hundreds of thousands of extra jobs to prove it.

The picture portrayed by Mr Kinnock is wholly different. Manufacturing investment is 21 per cent lower and output 6 per cent lower than this year of 1978, inflation soars higher in budget than at any time in history, and the tax burden 13 per cent higher than when Labour left office.

Both argue aged 35 who are diverted after the armed police strike of mismanagement, accuses his successor of a weakness of Kinnock Manchester in Royal Hospital for Nervous Diseases, in London, said yesterday that his counterpart

Stating that Britain enters 1986 with the future looking good, Mrs Thatcher says there is a return to clear beliefs and traditional values that she would most be agreed.

Mr Kinnock speaks of "an other year of decay under a get-away government that is selling off public assets, losing control and future income running public obligations, controlling wealth in fewer hands and making our country turn for seven twists on Sunday.

He was also accused of distancing to destroy his current House of Boards Bill.

Leading-article: page 13
Labour dismay: page 2

French fight for hostages' release

BY GEORGE GRAHAM

Travel agents offering package tours to the World Cup football matches in Mexico next June are taking precautions to ensure that, so far as possible, British football holidaymakers are eliminated from the terraces.

Advertisements have begun to appear in the Press offering all-in tours ranging from an 18-day package at £576 to see England, Scotland and Northern Ireland play their qualifying matches up to a three-week holiday for £1,800 to include the final.

About six tour companies are all with previous experience of overseas football packages, are offering tours to Mexico.

Mr David Dryer, of the Hove-based Holiday Shop company and an experienced travel consultant who worked on tours to the 1982 World Cup in Spain said yesterday that the companies involved would be checking the names of supporters who make bookings.

"The specialist tour companies have many regular clients whom they already know. But anyone unknown applying to join a package will have his address noted, and his name will be checked against lists of troublemakers held by football clubs in his own area. If he is a known troublemaker, obviously his booking will not be accepted", Mr Dryer said.

The travel industry expects about 8,000 British supporters to book package tours to Mexico, but it cannot over-emphasise how many will make their own arrangements to get there.

Vetting is likely to be particularly strict in Scotland where the several tours the Scottish Football Association has run its own travel agency and where, thanks to careful organisation, smaller numbers and legislation banning drink from grounds, hooliganism at football matches appears to have been brought under control.

The English Football Association does not have an agency. I don't see why a step forward by some back has happened today.

They had a perfectly adequate reception but the trade today, which cannot be attacked by a ticket for Mrs Thatcher "Every hour I must be busy and there satisfy these Their having so another point They seem to be doing that too.

The Prime Minister has not yet accepted Mr Heseltine's request for a special meeting of senior ministers to look again at the rival offers.

Mr Heseltine's supporters believe a meeting is necessary to compose a reply to Sir John Cuckney, Westland's chairman, who has written to the Prime Minister asking for clarification of the Government's defence procurement policy.

"A senior source said that Sir James Senior taken out to be answered collectively."

Prince Andrew, talking with workers after he opened the new Lancing, West Sussex, yesterday. He gave nothing away when aged 5, who was in the factory's cable section: "How's Fer..."

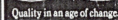

Quality in an age of change.

THE FAMOUS GROUSE
FINEST SCOTCH WHISKY

THE INDEPENDENT

News Summary

Brent Council social services committee last night sacked three staff for gross misconduct. This follows the inquiry into the death of a year-old Jasmine Beckford, whose stepfather has been jailed for her manslaughter. The dismissed social workers are Miss Gunn Wahlstrom, responsible for visiting the Beckford family, Mrs Diane Dietmann, a supervisor, and Mr William Thompson, principal social services officer for Brent Social Services in-between.

Mrs Jarrett's death accidental

Mrs Cynthia Jarrett's death, which sparked off the Tottenham riots in October, was accidental, an inquest jury in Haringey, north London, decided yesterday. The Jarrett family said the verdict was a vindication of their complaint against the police. Page 2 and 4

King apologises for Ulster gaffe

A chastened Mr King, Northern Ireland Secretary, expressed regret in a Commons statement for having suggested that Dr Fitzgerald, the Irish prime minister, had abandoned hope of a united Ireland. Page 2 and 5

Jaruzelski visit shocks France

The first visit by the Polish leader, General Jaruzelski, to a western head of Government since the imposition of martial law stirred substantial anger in France. President Mitterrand had to insist that the general entered the Elysée Palace by the back door. Page 1 and 8

Goal for animal rights activists

Seven animal rights activists were jailed for their "Robin Hood" raids on laboratories. Sentences handed down at Winchester Crown Court ranged from three years to nine months Page 3 and 1

NUM climbdown on productivity

Leaders of the National Union of Mineworkers may today decide to reverse last week's decision to oppose productivity deals. Some area committees have insisted upon a climb-down. Page 3 and 1

Flick Group for sale

West Germany's Flick Group is to be bought by the Deutsche Bank and sold on to investors. The deal is expected to value the privately owned group at a record DM 5 bn (£1.8bn).

Wall Street hits new peak

The Dow Jones average closed 25.94 points up at a record close of 1464.49 in New York. London share prices drifted lower. Page 13 and 1

Britain to leave UNESCO

Britain's withdrawal from UNESCO, the United Nations Educational, Scientific and Cultural Organisation, is expected to be announced today. Page 2 and 3

Union climb down

The Transport and General Workers Union is to ballot 57,500 Ford car workers on a strike call. This represents a softening of the union's hostility to the Government's new strike laws. Page 3 and 1

Reagan names new adviser

President Reagan announced the resignation of Robert McFarlane as US National Security Adviser and denied it was a result of a personality clash within the White House. Page 6 and 1

Plessey rejects GEC

Plessey turned down the £1.16bn bid approach made by General Electric Company and countered with a proposal to buy out GEC's interest in the System X digital telephone exchanges. Page 13 and 1

Scotland reaches soccer finals

Scotland drew 0-0 with Australia in Melbourne to secure it the 1986 World Cup finals places due to be played in Mexico next year. Page 24 and 1

Low pay equals low interest rates

Mr Lawson, chancellor of the Exchequer, told the National Economic Development Council that if management moderated wage increases, then lower interest rates would be more likely. 1 and 4

Downing Street celebration

The Queen and the Duke of Edinburgh joined Mrs Thatcher and five former prime ministers for dinner at No 10 Downing Street to celebrate the 250 years that have elapsed since the building first became prime minister's official residence.

Jaruzelski visit shocks France

Joe Kennedy stands for Congress

Joseph Kennedy, 33, eldest son of the murdered Senator Robert Kennedy and nephew of President John Kennedy, was standing in Dallas is to run for office. He is candidate for a Boston congressional district. Page 6 and 1

Bruno floors American

Frank Bruno, the European heavyweight champion from Wandsworth, knocked out Larry Frasier of the United States in the second round of a fight at the Royal Albert Hall in London Page 24 and 5

Delors welcomes EEC package

The hard fought EEC reforms agreed by Community leaders at the Luxembourg summit were welcomed by Jacques Delors, president of the European Commission. He said the package was "a compromise which means progress". Page 8 and 6

Weather Forecast

A depression will develop over the United Kingdom. England and Wales will be mostly cloudy with rain, heavy in places. Details on page 23

Council sacks three Jasmine workers

by Philip Stephens

Brent Council last night dismissed the three social workers involved in the Jasmine Beckford case less than 24 hours after the inquiry into the four-year-old girl's death had severely criticised their actions.

Miss Gunn Wahlstrom, the Swedish social worker who dealt directly with the Beckford family, Mrs Diane Dietmann, her Jamaican-born supervisor, and Mr William Thompson, the most senior of the three, were found guilty of gross misconduct.

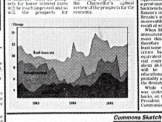

Lawson links interest to pay

by Robin Pauley

The Chancellor of the Exchequer yesterday appeared to offer industry the possibility of a bargain: if pay rises were to moderate, in turn rates could also come down.

Mr Nigel Lawson told the monthly meeting of the National Economic Development Council that the Government had no direct control over wage increases, but it did have responsibility for keeping down inflation. If pay accelerated, it was his duty to ensure that it did not feed through into higher inflation.

On the other hand, it was arguments followed the advice of the Confederation of British Industry and were warranted in reducing the level of settlements "then the prospects for lower interest rates will be much improved and so will the prospects for economy."

"I don't know the government run a supermarket"

Hugo Young on why the Church of England report, Faith in the City, embarrassed the government. Page 10

Michael Binyon on Robert McFarlane's departure from the White House. Page 12

Editorial Comment The Chancellor and interest rates. Page 12

Thatcher pulls Britain out of UNESCO

by Stephen Glover

The cabinet is expected to confirm today that Britain is to withdraw from Unesco at the end of the year on the grounds that the organisation remains wasteful and over politicised despite recent reforms.

The decision follows a strenuous campaign in Government circles, with most Foreign Office Ministers and Mr Timothy Raison, Minister for Overseas development, apparently still believing that Britain should stay and fight for change from within the organisation.

Against this view the Prime Minister has argued vigorously, with growing if reluctant support from her Cabinet colleagues, that the constitution of Unesco makes it impervious to reform.

Master King is whacked

by Godfrey Barker

It was Kinnock's study revisited yesterday. Enter an acquaintance, Mr Hurd was chastened, Master Tom King was whacked.

Injured dignity clung to the lad—not, as had been known much too against a whacking. King pretend not to be the fellow to brazen out his crime with the masters. But he did not whine for mercy either.

His time was of noble, elegiac regret, it did not save him MPs flews all around were adept at the pleasure ahead of a tremendous beating.

The Northern Ireland Secretary decided that Quoich might respond best to a grovelling apology.

"I spoke at lunch yesterday," he opened sorrowfully and irreverently, in sack in trouble do.

"I said that because the prin...

Jaruzelski enters by back door

by Stephen Glover

During a one day visit to Paris yesterday General Jaruzelski, the Polish leader, was made to enter the Elysée Palace via the back door, found it difficult to get a boat to carry him up the Seine and caused the French Prime Minister, M. Laurent Fabius, to fall out with President Mitterrand.

Scapegoats says NALGO

The dismissal of the three social workers brought an immediate threat of strike action by members of the National and Local Government Officers Association in Brent.

Mr Mike Trent, the local official for Nalgo, which has 3,100 members employed by the council, said last night that he was "confident" that a ballot would result in a decision to strike.

Quality in an age of change.

4) All sections of the newspaper, including the front page, would have summaries of the news which would then cross-refer to the complete story inside.

Hitchins: 'The idea of a front page news summary was there from the beginning and we were instructed to keep it at the top of the page despite similarity to the FT. We tried different positions but they were rejected.'

Much of Hitchins' early emphasis on large folio or page numbers and running headlines across the top of pages has survived the various stages of design, but not his choice of Castellar typeface. The idea of a chiselled masthead was carried through to launch but his choice of Franklin Gothic headlines and Nimrod text type (as now used by *The Guardian*) was later rejected.

Without acrimony, early in 1986 Hitchins moved on to other projects, leaving his designs behind. He was unfortunate perhaps because so much concentration was being given by the founders at that time to raising the second tier of finance.

Since January 1986, AWS had been trying to lure away the design editor of one of Fleet Street's most important newspapers. He proved elusive and on 9 May 1986, Ray Hawkey, the next designer, was commissioned. Hawkey had a strong background in newspapers and magazines, having been Art Editor of *Vogue* magazine, Design Director of the *Daily Express* and Presentation Director of *The Observer* and *Observer Colour Magazine*.

He was asked to work on a dummy issue that could be used for market research and began immediately. On 13 May, Tony Mullins, Art Editor of *The Observer*, was commissioned to work alongside Hawkey on this crucial test of market research. Time was vital. (By that time I had been offered a job on *The Independent* and was struggling to escape from Wapping.)

For several weeks I worked, alongside the few other journalists then at 40 City Road, with Hawkey and Mullins who were desperately trying to produce the second prototype. Hawkey's brief was vague. He knew that the newspaper was aiming at the 20-45-year-old ABC 1 market and that perhaps the newspaper ought to try to reflect that in some way. He was asked, like Hitchins before him, to place digests of news stories on most of the pages that began the sections. A lot of thought was being put into the design and presentation of the listings pages and television programmes.

At that stage the entire editorial complement, not counting the founders, numbered no more than ten, camping out on the third floor of the building with a few working telephones and a modicum of equipment. In a bare room, Hawkey organised paste-up tables and drawing boards. A rudimentary art department was being developed. Journalists came down from the floor above offering advice and probably hindrance too. I thought at that time I would end up on the design side but for the time being I was happy to help with planning any copy and photographs I could for the Hawkey/Mullins dummy. I started work at *The Independent* in the first week of June. I was asked to set up a temporary picture desk to research

The mood changes: a front page designed by Ray Hawkey and Tony Mullins – June 1986.

The Independent

FRIDAY MAY 16 1986   25p

PRINTED IN LONDON, MANCHESTER AND PORTSMOUTH

The
quick
brown
fox
P8

The
quick
brown
fox
jumped
P12

The quick brown fox
P16

The quick
brown fox
jumped
over
P19

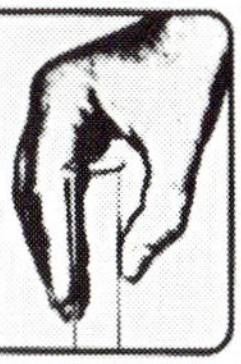

The
quick
brown
fox
P23

NEWS IN BRIEF

The quick brown fox jump

In the barge on the far right the actual one depicted by John Constable is one of his most famous paintings?

Archaeologists believe the huge timber shelt recovered from layers of mud on the River Stour is the remains of a boat depicted under construction in 'Boat Building near Flatford'.

The find has delighted 58-year-old John Constable, a great-great-grandson of the artist and a painter himself.

Mr Constable, who lives a few miles from Flatford, said: 'Most people now see Constable's pictures as romantic nostalgia about the English countryside.

The quick brow

In the barge on the far right the actual one depicted by John Constable is one of his most famous paintings?

Archaeologists believe the huge timber shelt recovered from layers of mud on the River Stour is the remains of a boat depicted under construction in 'Boat Building near Flatford'.

The find has delighted 58-year-old John Constable, a great-great-grandson of the artist and a painter himself.

Mr Constable, who lives a few miles from Flatford, said: 'Most people now see Constable's pictures

The quick brown fox ju

English countryside, but the barge painting shows that he was also interested in the industrial side of life.

Restoring the Flatford dock will give a touch of reality to Constable country for the visitors of today.

Work at the Suffolk site began after the National Trust, which owns the area, decided to restore the Suffolk

The quick brow fox jumped

In the barge on the far right the actual one depicted by John Constable is one of his most famous paintings?

Archaeologists believe the huge timber shelt recovered from layers of mud on the River Stour is the remains of a boat depicted under construction in 'Boat Building near Flatford'.

The find has delighted 58-year-old John Constable, a great-great-grandson of the artist and a painter himself.

Mr Constable, who lives a few miles from Flatford, said: 'Most people now see Constable's pictures

The quick brow

In the barge on the far right the actual one depicted by John Constable is one of his most famous paintings?

Archaeologists believe the huge timber shelt recovered from layers of mud on the River Stour is the remains of a boat depicted under construction in 'Boat Building near Flatford'.

Restoring the Flatford dock will

The quick

John Constable, a great-great-grandson of the artist and a painter himself.

Mr Constable, who lives a few miles from Flatford, said: 'Most people now see Constable's pictures

The quick brown fox ju

English countryside, but the barge painting shows that he was also interested in the industrial side of life.

Restoring the Flatford dock will give a touch of reality to Constable country for the visitors of today.

Work at the Suffolk site began after the National Trust, which owns the area, decided to restore the Suffolk

The quick brow fox jumped

Archaeologists believe the huge timber shelt recovered from layers of mud on the River Stour is the remains of a boat depicted under construction in 'Boat Building near Flatford'.

The find has delighted 58-year-old John Constable, a great-great-grandson of the artist and a painter himself.

The quick

Mr Constable, who lives a few miles from Flatford, said: 'Most people now see Constable's pictures

The quick brown fox

Restoring the Flatford dock will give a touch of reality to Constable country for the visitors of today.

Work at the Suffolk site began after the National Trust, which owns the area, decided to restore the Suffolk

The find has delighted 58-year-old John Constable, a great-great-grandson of the artist and a painter himself.

The quick

The quick brown fox ju

English countryside, but the barge painting shows that he was also interested in the industrial side of life.

Today's weather

AM   PM

Peacock says no to advertising on BBC TV

By John Smith Diplomatic Correspondent

Display caption: the quick brown fox jumped over the lazy dog

[body text in dummy filler repeating the Constable / Flatford article throughout the columns]

Storm over mortgage cuts to homeless

By John Smith Diplomatic Correspondent

The quick brown fox jumped

[line graph]

US weapon test fails

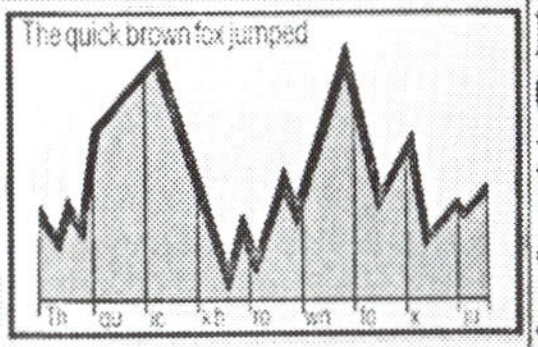

Divers brave Chernobyl radioactive waters

By John Smith Diplomatic Correspondent

Unemployment grows as factory output falls

By John Smith Diplomatic Correspondent

Pocket Cartoon
By Osbert Lancaster

"And should sixes of you be removed to write two numbers won't crossed one that all members of this Department are after for the industriously unacceptable and improper?"

and fill the dummy issue; no decision over a picture editor or design editor had been taken by then.

On 2 June 1986, Hawkey presented his first dummy pages (a front page, a centre-spread and a foreign news page).

It was an exciting moment. Hawkey had tried several different mastheads and experimented with Mullins on colour overlays on the front pages. His pages were bold and vivid and not at all in keeping with the other quality newspapers.

Despite some reservations from the working team, Hawkey and Mullins were asked to proceed with their 28-page specimen issue. The pressure increased. Journalists bearing rough copy would rush down to Hawkey who would then dispatch it to a firm of typesetters. They would return it later by messenger to Hawkey who would paste the setting on to the blank pages. It was a fascinating time. The newspaper was growing in front of us. Endless debates raged over the presentation and appearance while the few editors who had already arrived combined work on the dummy with a massive recruitment operation for their departmental staff.

I had joined *The Independent* as an Editorial Executive with the promise of a more specific job soon afterwards. I did further work on the dummy issue scheming out pages and then giving them to Hawkey and Mullins to make-up according to their new style. AWS wanted to experiment with colour on the front and back pages to test the appearance and to sample readers' opinion. I selected a very strong picture of a burning South African township for the front and a picture from Wimbledon of Jimmy Connors for the back. On 27 June, the final pages of the second prototype were delivered to the printers. On 2 July, they returned. We received 250 colour-printed copies and 250 black-and-white which were sent to Saatchi and Saatchi for the market research.

The feeling of elation was widespread. The journalists who had doubted the wisdom of having colour on the front page were won over by the superb reproduction. Of course, it was much better than we could normally expect, having been produced on a flat-bed lithographic press. It is worth considering here the style and typography used in this second prototype:

Headlines: Hawkey was asked to find a typeface that was not overtly dominant. Something that would be in keeping with the lengthy stories that were to appear in the newspaper. His search ended with Gibraltar. It is a condensed face that sits squarely on a page. The character or letter count is higher than one would normally expect and it comes in five different alphabetical appearances from a light design to a heavier black version. I had my doubts about its appeal as it seemed heavy and clumsy but others liked it.

By-lines: Here he preferred a fairly conventional sans serif face of Helvetica Bold. It is in widespread use and corresponds closely to what was eventually approved for final use.

Text: Most people agreed at that time that a Times-style typeface would be the best option. Hawkey and Mullins wanted to set

Variations on a theme: More front pages by Hawkey and Mullins – June 1986.

it 9pt type size on 10pt spacing condensed to a width value of 8pt. They thought it would give good legibility and clear leading through the lines. In the end we were to settle for a more straightforward version.

Pictures: Both Hawkey and Mullins were used to the general poor quality of photographic reproduction on Fleet Street newspapers and produced the dummy issue using a linear 50 line highlight drop-out. This put a heavy dot screen on the photographs and gave them a stark modern look that was more applicable to magazines. Some of them were also framed with 1pt rules. By that stage we had already decided on what was to be our future picture policy – bigger photographs than the other papers, with more feeling for the image behind the story (see chapters 7 & 8).

Rules: Normal vertical rules; a thick and a thin rule above and below the livery.

Masthead: The vital decision. Hawkey presented many mastheads of different sizes and typefaces, in different colours and in different positions.

Digests: Hawkey and Mullins never believed that the summaries would work on as many pages as had originally been planned. They thought a summary would dominate the front page and distract the readers from the rest of the page presentation.

Columns: Brief discussions had taken place over whether to opt for a nine- or even seven-column page but in the end conventional wisdom prevailed and an eight-column grid was agreed. It was really not so surprising when you consider that most broadsheet advertising comes in a fairly standard eight-column measure.

The printed dummy was initially well-received. AWS said he was 75 per cent happy with it. There were a few points which were not quite right. On 7 July an editorial meeting was held to examine the dummy and its future as a working model for *The Independent*. It was to prove momentous, considering that the plan was to produce papers under live conditions, starting at the end of August, for five weeks before the planned launch in October.

Here are some of the actual comments from the meeting:

On the front page – ' there was not enough room for stories, the picture should be smaller,' 'overall the colour picture worked well and didn't cheapen the paper,' 'large stories tended to look rather shabby.'

On page 2 (Home news) – ' the lines around the pictures made them look like library pictures and not newsy.'

On page 10/11 (Foreign news) – 'AWS liked graphic and felt it was right to have a map of Europe rather than a table. Nick Garland (the cartoonist), however, felt that the graphics on p.3, p.6 and p.10 were too elaborate for the story.'

On page 13 (Health Page) – ' typeface on the great drug dumping scandal didn't work. Problem of what to put with Gibraltar typeface – this one over ornate. Need to look at other typefaces.'

On page 23 (Arts Page) – 'rather bitty and lines too heavy. Felt to be least successful page,' 'pictures too large and too many.'

The eagles gather as the debate about the masthead continues. The top three are by Hawkey and Mullins; the bottom by Nicholas Thirkell.

THE INDEPENDENT

FRIDAY 13 JUNE 1986 — Published in London, printed in Peterborough, Bradford, Portsmouth and Sittingbourne — 25p

Hong Kong reactor study fails to reveal risks

Unionists in secret talks with King

Loyalist gunmen

By Peter Wilby

THE LARGEST teachers' union admitted defeat yesterday in its legal battle with employers over the obligation to cover for absent colleagues.

During the teachers' pay dispute, refusal to cover was one of the union's most effective tactics, which led to thousands of children missing lessons or dismissed early to teachers.

Leaders of the National Union

THE INDEPENDENT

FRIDAY 13 JUNE 1986 — Published in London, printed in Peterborough, Bradford, Portsmouth and Sittingbourne — 75p

Hong Kong reactor study fails to reveal risks

Unionists in secret talks

Loyalist gunmen

By Peter Wilby

THE LARGEST teachers' union admitted defeat yesterday in its legal battle with employers over the obligation to cover for absent colleagues.

During the teachers' pay dispute, refusal to cover was one of the union's most effective tactics

THE INDEPENDENT

FRIDAY 13 JUNE 1986 — Published in London, printed in Peterborough, Bradford, Portsmouth and Sittingbourne — 25p

Hong Kong reactor study fails to reveal risks

Unionists in secret talks with King

Loyalist gunmen

By Peter Wilby

THE LARGEST teachers' union admitted defeat yesterday in its legal battle with employers over the obligation to cover for absent colleagues.

During the teachers' pay dispute, refusal to cover was one of the union's most effective tactics which led to thousands of children missing lessons or dismissed early to teachers.

Leaders of the National Union

THE INDEPENDENT

No 1 — MONDAY 14 JULY 1986 — 25p

Brittan line gets backing in Cabinet

From our Correspondent in Johannesburg

Lord Pennock, joint chairman of the Euro Tunnel group, admitted yesterday that financial backers were raising difficulties.

Mr Jonathan Shoppett, chairman of the opposition Eurotevi consortium, said aspects of the scheme," Lord Pennock said.

would go through, and that banks were asking more questions about the prospectus than they had expected.

But he insisted that it was a matter of explanation rather than disagreement. The delay is simply because

News in brief

Jet crash

man of the Euro Tunnel group, admitted yesterday that financial backers were raising unexpected queries about the financing of the £6 billion Channel tunnel scheme due

Ferry aground

Roles, particularly in regard to capital cost, traffic forecasts, and tariff and interest rate assumptions, have been raised beginning

Among those present at the meeting were Alexander Chancellor, the US Editor of *The Independent* and former editor of *The Spectator*, and Nicholas Garland, the former *Daily Telegraph* cartoonist. They had played little or no part in the creation of this dummy but managed to persuade the meeting that all was not right with it. It is worth giving the summary of the basic points of this meeting because they set the seal for what was soon to be consolidated into the launch design – the fourth protocol:

☐ Overall on the right lines but . . .

☐ Alexander Chancellor raised point that the paper shouldn't be different for the sake of it. People like to feel comfortable with a paper and therefore shouldn't stray too far from the conventions of *Times/Guardian*. Masthead too bold and unsure whether typeface was right.

☐ Queried whether paper looked upmarket enough.

☐ Tom Sutcliffe's (Arts Editor) phrase 'classic with a twist' thought to aptly fit our aims.

Basic overall points:

☐ Consistency needed in digests/ summaries.

☐ Analysis should start with hard news point.

☐ Design problem distinguishing analysis/features/news.

☐ Lines, boldness, round corners.

☐ By-line positioning.

☐ Dates in repeated central columns, looks odd, typeface change?

☐ Screen on photos worked in some instances, not others.

☐ General appropriateness of graphics questioned.

The revisionists carried the day. Intense lobbying of AWS had taken place as some journalists began to feel that the printed dummy reflected the wrong image. It is extraordinary given the general approval of that dummy how decisively it was rejected.

We could not afford to wait for the results of the market research due on 1 August. It was back to the drawing board. Ray Hawkey left at that stage and Tony Mullins, who was still agonising over whether to leave *The Observer*, decided to carry on with a third prototype. Nick Garland introduced a friend of his, Nicholas Thirkell, of the design group Carroll, Dempsey and Thirkell, to AWS. It was decided to give them a chance to work with Tony Mullins on a new dummy.

At that stage the computer equipment was starting to arrive and it was vital to decide what typefaces to order for it. During the latter half of July a series of meetings were held between myself, Mullins, Thirkell and the salesmen who were to supply the ITC Bitstream typefaces.

There was still a lot of debate over the choice of headline typography. To cater for all tastes we ended up ordering several typefaces, most of which we never now use. I had already decided with the approval of AWS to opt for the text type that came with the Atex system – Dutch – or really Times New Roman with a marginally different cut. The size was to be $8\frac{1}{2}$ pt on 9pt setting which is what it remains today. I did a comparative test with type from *The Guardian*, *Times* and *Telegraph* to prove to AWS that the Dutch was both legible and word-effective.

Mullins was soon to leave to return to *The Observer*, saying that he had hoped AWS would wait for the result of the market research before proceeding any further. When it did arrive its findings were encouraging – the spontaneous reaction, of people sampled, to the dummy was that it was 'clean, crisp and inviting', ' a more modern design and format', 'designed to help the reader find his way around', 'major items broken up less than many broadsheets'. It was one of the few occasions when the newspaper was not influenced by market research and decided editorially that the dummy was wrong.

Thirkell's initial design did not fill me or most of the other journalists with much confidence. The headlines were very small, more akin to book design than newspapers. The photographs also were small, more in the style of *The Telegraph*. Initially only a couple of news pages were done. The layout and presentation seemed curiously out of place with no relationship between the weight and length of stories as they descended the page. The Oxford (thin and thick) rules were heavy. The masthead seemed too small and subdued for point-of-sale impact. AWS's wish for some sort of symbol, expressed months earlier, resulted in a beautiful eagle with every feather in place to the left of the masthead. It was the start of the eagle saga, more of which later.

The Carroll, Dempsey and Thirkell team departed again to return to their offices with only brief incursions into *The Independent*. 21 August was set aside as the day they would make the final presentation of a complete newspaper so we could start our dummy issues at the end of August. All this time I was busily trying to set up an art department and a picture department as well as working on the design. In July I had been appointed Executive Editor (Design and Pictures).

The meeting on 21 August proved a disaster. The Thirkell dummy was decisively rejected by AWS, Symonds, Glover, Nigel Lloyd and myself. AWS was to say later that it was the worst meeting he had had during the entire launch of the newspaper. Thirkell left to go on holiday and AWS asked me if I could redesign the newspaper in three days in time for the start of the vital dummy runs.

The London International Financial Futures Exchange during the Stock Market crash in October 1987. (Photo: Stewart Goldstein)

7: The Planning

The graphic design of a newspaper is not a
thing in itself. The good newspaperman does
not assemble type in a page merely to make
an agreeable pattern, or an exercise in
display for its own sake. Typography and
make-up in a newspaper are only a vehicle
for journalism.

Allen Hutt (1901–1973)

Typography, layout and photographs

During these difficult days of July and August when the design was
wavering from one end of the spectrum to the other, I was working
very closely with our operations staff and, in particular, Philip
Hollingbery who was brought in by Conaway specifically to write
formats into the computer system in accordance with the design
brief. It was one of the most stimulating periods of the build-up to
the launch of *The Independent*.

Time, as ever, was short and, because of the constant changes of
designers, the pressure to succeed was immense. The office by then
was gradually filling up, as more and more people left their
previous jobs to take the gamble and invest their talent, future and
often money in the newspaper. Equipment was being installed and
tested. Training classes were going on all over the building in the,
to most, unfamiliar technology. The carefully-designed desk
modules were in place. Grey carpet tiles were fixed on the floors,
red and black chairs started to arrive.

One day seemingly hundreds of red filing cabinets turned up in
pantechnicons. They were stacked up on the pavement and then
distributed around the offices, dazzlingly bright. Symonds said
proudly: 'I've ordered one for every member of the editorial staff.'

Every day we all learned more about setting up a newspaper. For
everyone it was new territory and, for the journalists, new technology. It was relatively easy for some people to pick up keyboard
skills and set their stories. Weeks after launch others were still
exhibiting the classic signs of technophobia and visibly shaking
when required to sit down and start their 'machines'. After my
experiences at Wapping where a similar Atex system was used, I
was somehow elected to the position of editorial keyboard wizard,
something which then and now I make no claim to. It fell upon me
to devise a system of passwords and 'logons' or signing-on names
to give journalists access to the mainframe computer system
through their own personal keyboards.

At Wapping the secret manoeuvres behind the commissioning of the newspaper plant had permeated every aspect of life there. For example, each journalist, on arrival, was handed a sealed white envelope. Inside it was his or her logon name plus a confidential never-to-be-disclosed password which gave access to the individual's personal queue. The confidentiality of both the passwords and the queues was soon to prove ridiculous. Knowing that at least someone, either a systems analyst or a senior production journalist, must have the secret password somewhere, destroyed any journalistic faith in the system. In fact, on the third day at Wapping, a journalist discovered the main computer file with everyone's logon name and secret password.

At *The Independent* it was to be different. The logon name was the first five letters of your surname and the open password was the first three of your Christian name. That system helped to stifle most of the anxieties that the large band of journalists had. Later some were to change their passwords but the system has basically remained unlocked and open.

During July and August, I spent a lot of time trying to work out a copy flow-chart for the computer operations staff. This was to show how many sources of different information would be required in each department electronically, i.e. the foreign department would receive copy from the wire agencies, Reuters, AP and UPI, into a computer 'queue' or, in other words, a large electronic filing cabinet. At the same time it would receive copy either telexed into the computer system, telephoned through to copy-takers or filed from portable pcs. Apart from that, writers based in the office would also be writing their stories into the foreign queue. Then the next stage was to arrange access for the various departmental editors to different parts of the system and to give them and the sub-editors the ability to interact electronically. Lastly, the tuning up of the GT68 layout machines in the light of the decisions taken concerning the above had to be done.

The fourth prototype:

The final design process of *The Independent* was broken up into four distinct but interrelated parts – layout, typography, graphics and computer programming. The first three are well-practised arts; the fourth, novel and fear-inducing.

Following the departure of Thirkell, who was to retain a limited contact with *The Independent* for a few weeks looking at possibilities for the centre-spread, the embryonic design department was left holding the pieces: pieces of layouts, typefaces, mastheads galore, rough graphics, typesheets, examples of rule work, quite a few eagles. The skill and experience of Michael McGuinness, who was soon to join us full-time as Deputy Art Editor, proved invaluable over the weeks and months to come.

Because time was so short, something had to be made ready in a matter of days for the first dummies and something concrete in a matter of weeks, I had to act fast with the help of AWS and his co-founders and shake the pieces into some sort of coherent order that would work in design terms and also be translated into viable computer layouts.

Layout:

I was very conscious of the fact that although we had run the gamut of typefaces from old to new and back again and spent an inordinate time on mastheads, the actual details of layout had not ever been pinned down. Was it to be full modular layout like *The Times* of the 1970s and beyond? Was it to be irregular like *The Guardian* news pages? Was it to be static like *The Telegraph* where a template is used with little change, or dynamic like *The Observer*?

The sub-divisions grow; *The Times* is modular – its headlines and stories form rectangular or square blocks; *The Telegraph* is irregular but its headlines are modular, i.e; they do not spill from one column width to another.

The questions lay heavy on the mind. How would the weight and size of the headline typography we eventually agreed on affect the overall decisions regarding layout? Where would the use and choice of photographs fit into the equation? Where should by-lines be placed?

Evans had summed up the common problem neatly: 'The philosophy of functional newspaper design inevitably means that many of the design solutions cannot be suggested in advance of the problem. It does not mean however that there are not principles to guide both layout policy and the inspiration of the moment. There are. They spring from the purpose of page design. Organisation is the first expectation.'

Modular layout, it is true, organises the presentation of news items, in particular, into attractive self-contained elements. It imposes a discipline on the page designer, the sub-editor and the writer to work within a framework of consistency. Headlines slot naturally into place both for the designer and the reader. Text follows the dictates of the headline, running smoothly below without undue and unseemly breaks. True modular layout adds to the discipline by stopping turning material. *The Times* has abandoned earlier practice and lost a degree of its design superiority by turning stories from the front page to the back page.

The advantages are clear. The disadvantages are less apparent to the reader or often the writer – a layout artist or sub-editor might artificially squeeze or enlarge the space given to a particular story in order to fit his module or rectangle.

Modular layout was therefore the *sine qua non* of *The Independent* with its ordered and organised news flow. A structured layout for a structured newspaper.

I prefer to call the developed layout style of *The Independent*, semi-modular. As in most areas of the newspaper, there is freedom to manoeuvre within a strict framework. Some layouts do not align with the advertisements in precise rectangles. Some stories do wrap around others. (On pages with no advertisements, such as the

Gazette page, I was conscious of the need to bring the eye down the page when faced with such large areas of small, detailed and grey type.)

Having arrived at the semi-modular look to the layout, the next step was the organisation within that in terms of importance and emphasis. It would be out of keeping with the custom and practice of British newspapers to allow a page to contain several headlines of the same point size or several stories of similar length. One of the major problems with some of the earlier dummies had been the lack of thought that went into the relationship between headlines and stories as they descended the page. The danger was to go too far the other way; Evans again: 'Newspapers . . . do not seem to appreciate that emphasis is a matter of relativity. The whisper in the quiet room is as emphatic as the shout in a hubbub. If every headline shouts there is no emphasis . . . . It is this failure to realise that all display is no display that combines so frequently with severely irregular layout to transform a humble enough newspaper into a Kafkaesque confusion.' We had been warned, not only by Evans but by our past experience of a number of newspapers.

In any aspect of design, it is always tempting to allow undue experimentation before returning to the straight and narrow path trod by generations of newspaper layout men before. At that stage we didn't have the time to experiment but followed normal style in terms of headline type size: The page lead headline was in 60pt, the second story in 48 or 42pt, the third and subsequent stories in 36pt, 30pt, 24pt etc in descending scale. Some variation was provided at an early stage by a very strong emphasis on anchor or basement stories which sit on the bottom of a page, often in a different column-width and in bold type.

Computer note 1: *The Independent* is made up on screen on the basis of 9pt line spaces. The hidden grid determines exactly how the layout and headlines fit on to it. For weeks there was a debate over whether to have a gridded or ungridded system which would allow more flexibility in point size variation but also cause severe difficulties in computer terms. The 9pt gridded system means that all the elements of that page, the headlines, the text size etc should be divisible by 9. This means that although headlines are called in the conventional way, ie, 60pt, 48pt, 42pt etc, their actual size depends on their relationship to a certain number of 9pt lines.

To an extent this design formula was confirmation of what the people primarily concerned with day-by-day layout were used to on their previous newspapers – mainly *The Times*, *Telegraph*, *Observer*. It was the formalisation of a style that was so important. Like most other things during the end of August and September, these decisions were taken on the run and through a number of dummy pages.

Along with the form of layout (semi-modular) and the gradation of headlines from top to bottom, the placing of art, both pictures and graphics, was the next most important principle behind the layout. (I will deal more fully with the photographic development

Another early front page produced at the newspaper – 28 August 1986.

THE INDEPENDENT

Published in London 25p THURSDAY 28 AUGUST 1986

Police kill 12 as rent riots sweep Soweto

By Tony Allen-Mills, Johannesburg

THE BLACK South African township of Soweto was last night mourning the deaths of at least 12 people killed by police in one of the worst nights of violence since the Government imposed a state of emergency last June.

A thirteenth man, a Soweto town councillor, was hacked to death by a mob and unofficial sources in the township claimed the death toll could rise to more than 20.

The rioting erupted amid protests by black demonstrators over the eviction of Soweto families from their homes for council rent arrears.

Local residents and the government's Bureau for Information gave differing versions of how exactly the trouble started, but the bureau acknowledged that police opened fire on protesters soon after arriving at the scene.

An official statement on the violence said police in three Land Rovers drove into the White City area of Soweto to investigate a roadblock of burning tyres.

"When the police arrived at the scene, they were confronted by a large group of blacks", the statement said.

"A grenade was thrown at the police, exploding between two of the Land Rovers and injuring one white and three black members (of the police). The police then fired at the group."

The bureau said seven blacks were killed on the spot and an eighth died later in hospital. In a separate incident, police shot four more blacks dead at another roadblock in Mphefu Avenue, Soweto.

Despite government reports of 69 wounded in the incidents, a spokesman at the Baragwanath hospital who did not wish to be identified told an Agence France-Presse reporter that more than 100 had been hurt.

The renewed outbreak of violence shocked many whites who were last week assured by government ministers that the state of emergency and mass detentions of black activists had successfully reduced unrest in the townships.

The roots of Tuesday night's violence appeared to stem from tension over the black rent boycott and local council eviction policies.

The Government estimates that tens of thousands of pounds in rent revenues have been lost to the boycott. In the last week, at least five families said to be owing the Soweto Town Council "substantial" sums in arrears have been forcibly removed from their homes.

The appearance in Soweto on Tuesday of teams of council police ready to carry out further evictions was reported by several township residents to have sparked off the new round of violence.

Much of the protesters' wrath was aimed at Black Soweto councillors considered party to the eviction policy. Mr Sydney Sideshe Mkwanazi was reported to have died in hospital after being set upon by a group of youths. Another councillor, Mr Sighrid Matshata, fled with his family from his home in Naledi as angry demonstrators set it on fire.

Last night Soweto was reported tense but quiet. Earlier in the day council police used tear gas to disperse a group of about 500 people who marched on council offices to protest the evictions. A spokesman for the Bureau for Information said later violence had fizzled out and there were "only a few incidents of stone-throwing" being reported. "This is nothing out of the ordinary", he said.

The latest deaths brought the toll from ten weeks of unrest since the state of emergency was declared to more than 200.

● The archbishop of the largest Catholic diocese in the United States, Cardinal Joseph Bernardin of Chicago, has protested to the Pretoria government over the detention and alleged torture of a senior Catholic priest.

The cardinal said in a telegram to the South African ambassador that detention and harassment of church workers was an unacceptable moral outrage.

The protest was prompted by the detention of the Rev. Smangaliso Mkhatshwa, general secretary of the South African Bishop's Conference, who is reported to have been physically abused in custody.

● CAPE TOWN: Cape Town's white liberal council said yesterday it would give a dinner for controversial foreigners invited by Bishop Desmond Tutu to his enthronement as archbishop of the city next month.

White conservatives have strongly protested over the guest list, which includes prominent advocates of sanctions against Pretoria.

The local tourist board said it would offer the visitors a whistle-stop sight-seeing tour, taking in beaches reserved until last year for whites.

Conservative newspapers have launched vituperative attacks on the bishop for inviting politicians and entertainers to the ceremony on September 7.

Mrs Winnie Mandela visits the area in Soweto yesterday where 12 rent protestors were killed in clashes with police.

Row over inadequate four years for street rapist

By Robert Rice

SIR JAMES Miskin, Recorder of London yesterday sentenced a rapist to only four years imprisonment at the Old Bailey because the attack took place in the street and had none of the "beastliness" of cases where rape was committed during burglary or weapons were used.

The sentence, which ignores the guidelines on rape sentences laid down by Lord Lane, the Lord Chief Justice, earlier this year, was attacked by both the victim's family and the police as totally inadequate in view of the violence of the assault and the fact that the rapist had given the victim venereal disease.

The leniency of the sentence is bound to add to the recent controversy on the inadequacy of rape sentences. Last week, Peter Bruinvels, Conservative MP for Leicester East, called for castration of rapists and a minimum 30 year prison sentence for persistent offenders.

Although a sentence of life imprisonment for rape is available to the courts it is rarely used. The average sentence given for rape is two to five years.

The sentencing guidelines issued by the Lord Chief Justice in February call for a minimum of five years imprisonment for adult rapists pleading guilty without mitigating circumstances. But it seems that the courts are largely ignoring them.

In sentencing Wayne Scott, Sir James said that he could not pass a lighter sentence because he pleaded guilty only at the "11th hour and 59th minute" forcing the victim to live the last 11 months of her life "on the basis that she would have to go into the witness-box and relive her ordeal".

The incidence of rape is rising steadily according to Home Office statistics. There were 1,842 convictions for rape in 1985 compared with only 1,068 in 1981.

The increase can be partly explained by a greater willingness of victims to report rapes following a much publicised campaign by the police to present a more caring approach to the treatment of rape victims. But many women believe that the apparent increase in the number of rapes merely reflects a slow realisation of the size of the problem of violence against women in this country.

Discrepancies in sentences given by the courts for rape have done nothing to reassure women that the problem is taken seriously by a male-dominated judiciary.

In July an unemployed labourer was jailed at Reading Crown Court for a total of seven years after he admitted raping a 14 year old schoolgirl and committing 250 sexual offences against young women on a university campus in the space of three weeks.

In May a former psychiatric patient who tried to rape an 18 year old woman 11 months after he was released from Rampton special hospital was sentenced to two life sentences. And in June a man who had drunk 30 pints of lager before committing the crime was given an 18 month sentence at the Old Bailey after the judge told him that he had never heard of a man drinking that much and remaining conscious let alone being able to do what he had done.

Of the 95 per cent of rapists who received custodial sentences in 1984, 28 per cent received sentences of two years or less; 23 per cent over two and up to three years; 18 per cent over three and up to four years; 18 per cent over four and up to five years; and eight per cent over five years including two per cent who received life sentences.

Crack arrives in Britain

By Sarah Helm

CRACK, the cocaine-based drug, has appeared in Britain for the first time. Voluntary agencies are reporting a small number of cases, so far confined to the London area.

Mr David Turner, coordinator of SCODA, an umbrella organisation for voluntary drug abuse bodies, said yesterday that the appearance of crack coincided with a marked increase in cocaine abuse throughout the country.

"A number of our agencies are now reporting a greater availability of cocaine. We are seeing the drug in areas of the country where it was previously almost nonexistent."

Crack, a particularly lethal variation of cocaine, has recently swept America and is already beginning to take a hold on the continent.

A mixture of cocaine powder, baking soda and water, it is smoked in pipes and is more addictive than ordinary cocaine. It also gives a quicker high.

Experts fear a growth in the use of crack because it can be bought in smaller and therefore cheaper quantities. Straight cocaine is normally sold by gramme weights in £50-£70 quantities. Reports reaching SCODA suggest that crack is being sold in London in £10 weights.

"At the moment the use of crack is still very limited but we predict that it could become a serious problem within 6-12 months if it becomes widely marketed at street level," said Mr Turner.

The government's fight against drug abuse has increasingly focused on cocaine in recent months with growing evidence that South American drug traffickers have now saturated the American market and are turning their attentions on Europe. Police in Britain and throughout Europe are reporting a steady increase in the number of arrests of South Americans for drug trafficking offences. The countries being most widely used by cocaine traffickers are Spain, Portugal and West Germany.

Some recent arrests suggest that traffickers may be switching their tactics, aiming at smuggling bulk quantities through freight ports rather than using individuals to smuggle the drug through airports.

Intelligence officers in Britain are also anticipating moves by the South Americans to infiltrate organised crime.

NEWS INDEX HERE

?

Carriers' exercise 'routine'

By John Bulloch

THE AMERICAN aircraft carriers Forrestal and America continued their much-publicised manoeuvres in the eastern Mediterranean yesterday, but in Washington officials indignantly denied that they were trying to put pressure on Col Gaddafi.

Defence Department officials said the deployment was "strictly routine" and had nothing to do with the situation in Libya. This was in contrast to a previous statement, which said that the Forrestal had been diverted from a planned visit to Israel as a demonstration of American willingness to take action against Libya if the need should arise.

The Libyans reacted as they did before last April's bombing attacks — by inviting representatives of the world media to see for themselves that Tripoli was quite normal, and that the leader was as he usually is.

In Washington last night all was injured innocence. The carrier America was not really part of the manoeuvres at all, the officials said, and was in fact on its way to Spain.

Even the much-heralded trip to Europe by General Vernon Walters, the American Ambassador to the UN, was played down.

Gaddafi — business as usual

In London, the American Embassy and the Foreign Office both said they hoped the General would be meeting Sir Geoffrey Howe. The Foreign Office hoped, too, that General Walters would be able to provide some reasons for the sudden American warning of possible new Libyan terrorist attacks.

Finally, "a high administration official" tried hard to dismiss all that had gone before. The original article in the *Wall Street Journal* which had started all the fuss was "misguided, unauthorised, and a premature effort on the part of some people in the administration to stimulate anti-Libyan feelings," he said.

All in all, the Reagan administration seemed to have a lot of egg on its face. At the same time, it seemed worth noting that the official put up to deny all that had gone before did speak of premature disclosure. It could be that everything was right except the timing of the leak.

● Eighteen American F-111 aircraft flew into Britain last night but the Pentagon denied the move had any connection with Libya.

TSB share issue attracts over 2.7 million inquiries

By Peter Wilson-Smith

TRUSTEE Savings Bank Group, which is set to raise more than £1bn by selling shares on the stock market next month, has been inundated with inquiries from the public but investors will have to wait two more weeks for final details of the share issue. The timetable for the issue, the biggest stock market flotation in this country outside the government's privatisation programme, was disclosed yesterday in a pathfinder prospectus.

The pathfinder is a final draft of the prospectus with all the details except the price at which shares in TSB Group are to be sold. This will be announced on 12 September and investors wanting to buy shares will have to apply by the morning of 24 September.

Lazard Brothers, the merchant bank handling the sale, revealed yesterday that 2.7 million people had asked for information about the flotation.

TSB Group has set a target of attracting more than 1 million shareholders. Interest in the share sale from the public is at present running at a higher level than at the same stage in run up to the British Telecom flotation. British Telecom initially attracted more than 2 million shareholders although the number has since fallen to about 1.7 million.

In the pathfinder prospectus TSB Group is predicting a 14 per cent increase in profits to £193 million before tax in the year to 20 November.

Although the pricing and the amount to be raised is not being disclosed yet, Lazard Brothers said they expected the shares to yield at least 5.5 per cent at the offer price.

Half of the shares being sold are being reserved for customers and staff of the bank, who will have priority when they apply for shares, providing they register by 5 September. TSB Group staff will also be able to apply for about £150 of free shares.

The minimum investment will be about £400 for members of the public and about £200 for those who qualify for priority applications. However initially investors will only have to pay over half these sums because payment will be in two instalments a year apart.

In order to encourage investors to keep their shares, a loyalty bonus will be paid after three years.

Business and Finance, page 17

Shorts workers stage walkout after flags ban

From our Correspondent, Belfast

WORKERS AT the Short Brothers aircraft factory in Belfast walked out yesterday afternoon, less than a week after management banned displays of "loyalist" flags and emblems in the plant. At least half the plant's 7,000 workers were thought to be involved in the action.

Loyalist flags and posters were still displayed at the factory despite last Friday's letter from the company chairman, Sir Philip Foreman, to all employees, saying they must be taken down "forthwith" on pain of disciplinary action.

The Orange Order in Belfast warned of possible industrial action and the Democratic Unionist Party leaders the Rev Ian Paisley and Peter Robinson were negotiating with workers and management to try to prevent a strike. The company refused to say how many people were still working. There was no picket line.

Sir Philip's letter came after Catholic employees — about 10 per cent of the workforce — said their clocking-on cards were removed and torn up, and the Loyalist Workers' Committee warned them to stay away from the factory.

Earlier this week, Shorts said it might allow several more days before all the display items must be removed. Officials pointed out that there was a factory floor area of more than two million square feet to be examined.

Shorts denied loyalist claims that the company was were under pressure from the Northern Ireland Office to impose the ban.

In an effort to avoid industrial action, Mr Robinson said: "We have put some proposals before the directors and indicated that we would put these same proposals before a representative group of men and would then go back to management for a further meeting."

The two DUP leaders said they had learned that the ban did not cover photographs of the Queen, although it did include displaying the Union Jack.

Labour goes for 'green' vote

THE LABOUR Party yesterday unveiled its environment programme which is aimed at securing the "green" vote at the next election.

A new ministry of environmental protection, tighter controls on industrial pollution, hazardous chemicals, food additives and land use and a ban on fox and stag hunting are proposed. Labour also plans to impose rates on agricultural land and buildings.

Dr John Cunningham, the Shadow Environment Secretary, said that two new agencies would be created to enforce the measures. This would include the monitoring of other Whitehall departments. The environmental protection service would supervise food hygiene and support research into pollution. The wildlife and countryside service would implement new protection legislation. The proposals were welcomed by the Council for the Protection of Rural England and the Ramblers Association.

John Gummer, the Agriculture Minister, said the rating proposals would mean higher food prices.

● Green revolution, Page 4

Sprint gold for Christie at Stuttgart

LINFORD CHRISTIE, 26, of London won the 200 metres gold medal at the European Athletics Championships in Stuttgart last night. His victory was Britain's first in this event in the championships for 40 years. Alan Wells of Scotland was fifth. Daley Thompson, the undisputed champion of the decathlon for the last decade, is in danger of losing his European title to Jurgen Hingsen.

Report — Back page.

AITHUPIAD

of *The Independent* in the following chapter.) It is the convention on broadsheet newspapers to place a photograph on the immediate right of the page lead and main headline. This is still a custom that *The Times*, *The Guardian* and *The Daily Telegraph* maintain slavishly apart from that imprecise special occasion. Not only is the photograph placed there, it is all too often cut or channelled into a specific size; in the case of *The Times* and *The Telegraph* a three column photograph by between 10 and 15 cms deep.

This attitude while admittedly providing an atmosphere of regular and ordered calm, contradicts the essence of news photographs and stories – that they are only selected out of a huge database, basket, file, call it what you will, because they are new and therefore of information and interest to the reader. To slot news and photographs into predetermined holes is to treat the reader with some contempt and to deny the layout artist his skill. Formula layout can work in certain circumstances but is to be resisted as a matter of principle. Consistency of format is much more important, that is placing regular items in the same place on the same page in the same position in the newspaper. If you place the crossword on the bottom left-hand side of the back page, it should stay there. The two practices are often confused and seen as synonymous.

The placing of a photograph in the specified position on the front page arose from the necessity on the quality papers, during their long and painful evolution, to separate the headlines. A photograph placed thus is often thought to be in the optical centre of the page providing balance on each side. But is it and does it? I doubt it.

The optical centre of a page is, Evans tells us, in the mathematical centre of the page as a vertical unit but not in the horizontal. It is therefore one-third of the distance from the top. It follows from there that one should place the optical centre of a photograph over the optical centre of the page to achieve the perfect optical balance. This might work well with so-called symmetrical layout but this mathematical formula restricts the use of well-taken photographs and provides little visual excitement for the reader. He or she may be drawn to the photograph because of its position but may well not register its content both because he or she expects a photograph to be there and because photographs are usually spoilt by cramming them into preconceived shapes and sizes. It would be like cutting a fine painting to fit a picture frame rather than the other way round.

The build-up to and the production of the first dummies enabled us to experiment with much bigger photographs than usual on broadsheet newspapers and to place them in unconventional positions on a page. This flexibility of approach was stimulating. People were breaking out of their layout moulds. If a picture looked better on the left-hand side of a page or on the right and still worked in relation to the other elements around it, it could be placed there. If a picture helped to hold up the bottom of the page, it could be placed there. The rule was that there was no fixed rule about placing photographs; they were to be treated on their merits each time a layout was done. That did not mean that there was unstructured layout. Of course, we got it wrong many times but by a couple of weeks before launch the photographic formula was in place in most sections of the newspaper.

As before, a lot of the background stimulus for layout philosophy came from AWS. He remained unable, in design jargon terms, to identify precisely what he wanted but everyone knew when he did not like something. Symonds who had had some basic layout experience from his training as a journalist was sure that the Hawkey dummy was wrong when it first appeared. He felt that if the newspaper appeared like that the editorial content would somehow be different. He was convinced that there had to be a relationship between content and style of presentation.

Computer note 2: *The Independent* does have the capability to scan photographs through its computer typesetting system directly onto the page. In practice it takes too much memory and the results are less predictable than through the use of a bromide-making machine for pasting onto the page.

The final decisions about typography remained to be taken:

Typography:

During the course of the dummies the headline typography went from Franklin Gothic, to Gibraltar, to Clarendon and to Century. My first task was to consolidate. Did Century really work on a properly made-up full page with everything in place? There was no way of telling, since the typeface had not arrived to be inserted into our computer system. I sent mock headlines outside to typesetters and got back a variety of point sizes all in Century for pasting up. My reservations about it were shared by other executives in the office. Some said it looked dull and lacked pace for news stories. Others felt it was exactly in keeping with the way they perceived the design ending up. The debate raged on until AWS in his usual decisive way as time dwindled said: 'It must be Century. It is the only acceptable option.'

I was determined to get the headlines on news pages ranged left; I felt it made them much stronger and more newsy. Another debate ensued, friendly yet challenging. Headlines in the non-printed dummies were ranged left. We had to see everything as though it were for real before a decision based on experience could be reached.

The first printed dummy was due out on the night of Monday, 1 September. Until two days before that we were producing pages using the text type of Dutch (Times) as the headline type. Once again everything seemed to arrive as close to the deadline as could be.

The choice of type for by-lines was a simpler decision. 11pt Helvetica Bold for the name and Medium for the title. My original design brief shows that by-lines were to have a 1pt rule above and a 2pt rule below and be set left. Eventually the rules were changed to a 1pt rule top and bottom and the by-lines became centred when just days before launch we decided to opt for centred headlines.

On captions, after much earlier flirtation with a sans serif face, we settled on a bold font for our text. In $8\frac{1}{2}$pt for single column captions and $9\frac{1}{2}$pt for anything more than three columns. With a few minor variations, most of which came later during the launch period and after, we have kept to simple typographical variations. (When I was asked to come up with an acceptable form of setting for classified advertisements, both in numbers of characters and words per line and lines per centimetre, Clarendon, the earlier headline favourite, emerged the clear winner.)

The masthead was still giving us problems. We had all seen so many that it was extremely difficult to make an absolute choice. About this time, Tom Sutcliffe's description of what *The Independent* layout should perhaps be – 'classic with a twist' was becoming a very useful yardstick. In the end we returned to the beginning and the original idea of Hitchins for a chiselled masthead and an idea subsequently repeated by Thirkell. However, all the previous versions seemed wrong in some way and I asked Michael McGuinness if he knew of someone who could hand draw a new version. He did and the present masthead drawn by Ken Dyster of the Mike Reid Studios in in-line Bodoni is unique.

Graphics:

For many reasons the establishment of the graphics side of the equation was to prove one of the most interesting and innovative parts of the entire design exercise. When I was originally asked to set up the design department, I began to think in conventional terms of artists drawing by hand, getting type set on the computer, and doing elaborate paste-up; a traditional way of producing maps, charts, tables etc. However we were to take a very different path. David Hewson, a friend of mine who also left *The Times* to join *The Independent*, was a keen user of personal computers both for word-processing and their graphic capabilities. He had recently acquired an Apple Macintosh and a Laserprinter which enabled him to produce his own magazine called *The Wordsmith* in his study in Kent. He convinced me that because there would be no union problems in any aspect of the new technology, I should try to set up a graphics 'work station' as it has now become known. The more I explored the feasibility of computer-generated graphics, the more I was sure that we could be in the forefront of a desk-top publishing revolution.

We had one Apple Mac and managed to find two freelance computer artists who were available to work part-time. From nothing we built up a style and design for graphics, initially mainly for the Business and City pages, but later for all departments of the newspaper, especially where maps were required. As we progressed, more and more software came onto the market and we were able to experiment with it to see if it fitted our needs.

The ease of use, the speed of operation and the clarity of the end

Some examples of the use of Apple Macintosh computers to produce maps, graphics and logos.

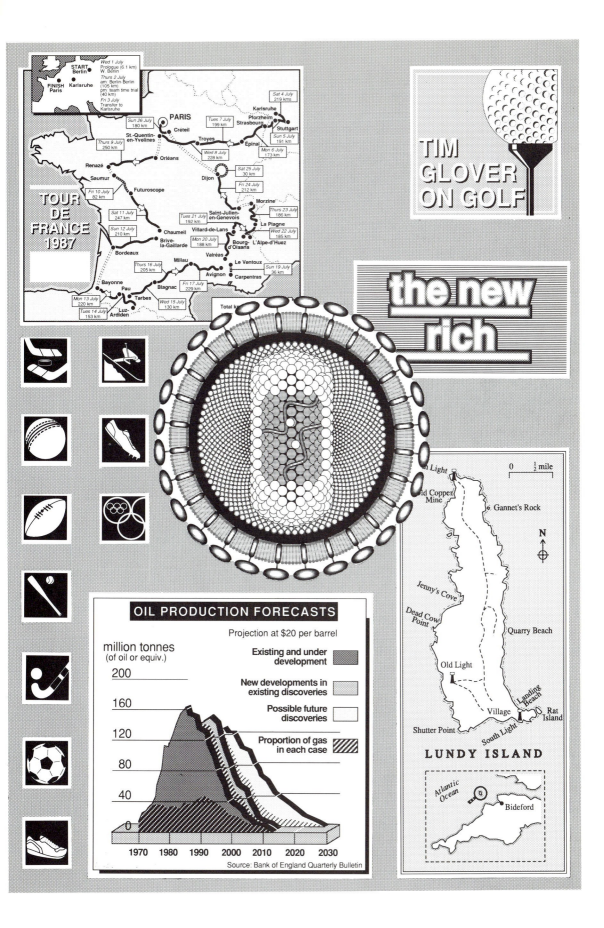

TOUR DE FRANCE 1987

TIM GLOVER ON GOLF

the new rich

OIL PRODUCTION FORECASTS

Projection at $20 per barrel

million tonnes
(of oil or equiv.)

200
160
120
80
40
0

Existing and under development
New developments in existing discoveries
Possible future discoveries
Proportion of gas in each case

1970 1980 1990 2000 2010 2020 2030

Source: Bank of England Quarterly Bulletin

LUNDY ISLAND

Old Copper Mine
Gannet's Rock
Jenny's Cove
Dead Cow Point
Quarry Beach
Old Light
Landing Beach
Village
Rat Island
Shutter Point
South Light

N

0   ½ mile

Atlantic Ocean
Bideford

product soon convinced all but the most reactionary that this was the way to proceed. The Crozier formula emerged: 'Half the number of people can produce three times as many graphics at one-third the normal cost in half the time.'

For mechanical artwork, the ability to experiment with headline typography, for the capacity to act as a database for the storage and retrieval of graphic material, a personal computer system easily outweighed conventional methods. We were not to know the true strength at that time. We still had traditional artists working in the design department helping with a lot of graphic material, layouts and caricatures. Even the most modern department will need their services.

The typography of the graphics was more problematical as only a certain number of typefaces was available at the time for the pcs. We settled on a form of Helvetica for the graphics, which remain the only part of the newspaper where the use of white headlines reversed out of black or WOBS are allowed – each day on the Business pages on statistical charts.

As these crucial weeks progressed constant efforts were made to refine the graphic techniques and style. As on the general keyboard side and as with the on-screen layout, we were all having to come to terms with new technology quickly. There was no stepping back and saying: 'Hang on a minute, I'm used to doing things this way.' Those times were past times.

Computer programming:

During this period, the journalists designated GT68 layout operators were being trained to use their layout screens. As the design briefs emerged, they were translated by a number of people, but mainly Hollingbery, into formats. Existing software was constantly being upgraded to match the demands of the journalists and the system.

My approach was as follows: On normal layout paper I would make-up a page with paste-ups of type either set in galley form in our computer room or outside the office by private typesetters. Beginning at the top of the page, I would paste down or draw an initial horizontal rule, then after careful spacing insert the folio or page number and another rule. Then more space would be added before the start of the headline, and also before the by-line and the start of the text. A picture might come next with space above and below it and its caption and the rule below that. When visually and artistically the page looked right, I would pass it on to Hollingbery who would work his magic on the computer and write an easily-identifiable format to reproduce the make-up.

It was a tedious but exciting process. There were only a few days left before the first printed dummies would go to the waiting panel of test readers. It would not help our market research or the prospects for launching on 7 October if the product was still a test-bed prototype. Everyone in the design department felt under great pressure to get it right in time for D-Day or Dummy Day.

Hollingbery would spend hours tapping away at his keyboard, inputting line after line of computer language to write a format for a rule or headline. He was meticulous in organising his formats to allow for all the possible variations that layout can produce. Some were so complicated as to baffle the in-house computer experts. Late in the evening he would come to find me, clutching the latest piece of galley. In his quiet way he would say: ' I think I've cracked it now, Mike. Here's that by-line you wanted.' He would then wander away back to his keyboard. Only later did I appreciate just how much work he put into making the design work on those computers.

The opening of Musée D'Orsay in Paris after refurbishing in
November 1986. (Photo: Brian Harris)

8: Countdown to Launch

He that will write well in any tongue
must follow this counsel of Aristotle
to speak as the common people do, to
think as wise men do; and so should
every man understand him, and the
judgement of wise men allow him.

Roger Ascham (1515–1568)

Numbers were building up. The great vacuum of the empty office was being filled. On 18 August another 28 journalists arrived bringing total editorial staffing up to 122. The keyboards were becoming operational as the highly-complicated wiring was channelled between floors. All round the building little pockets of journalists clustered around their keyboard trainers. For those who had left Wapping, the keyboard was familiar, although some functions were different. On the faces of some of those just starting, there were looks of desperation as they realised that the day of the typewriter was over for them. Some kept typewriters and would disappear into isolated corners to type out a story before finding somebody to key it into the system or show them how to do it. Many felt that stories would be lost if they turned off their VDTs, and left them switched on at night.

Some key positions, even at that late stage, were still to be filled, especially those of sub-editors. Secretaries and advertising staff were arriving, circulation men were being taken on. A canteen was emerging in the basement. The photographic darkroom was taking shape and the photographers were assembling. Setting up the picture desk caused many problems, all of which were overcome in one way or another. I was able to approach photographers I had come across on other newspapers or magazines and offer them something very new on *The Independent*. The philosophy had once again been articulated by AWS; it was my job to implement it.

He had made no secret of his admiration for *La Repubblica, Libération* and *El Pais*. He was particularly impressed by the way *Libération* used pictures very large and atmospherically. He said shortly before launch: 'I am wholly against the traditional cropping of pictures. With a shot of Mrs Thatcher meeting businessmen at 10 Downing Street, for example, I would include some background of 18th century furnishing that is the only interesting thing about the place. This, of course, is foreign to all journalistic canons of cropping which say that you have to concentrate on the faces and steer into the main point of the picture.'

I knew that the original three staff photographers, Brian Harris,

John Voos and David Ashdown, and the three contract photographers, Suresh Karadia, Herbie Knott and Jeremy Nicholl, were frustrated by the lack of attention given by newspapers to decent photographs. They belong to a generation weaned on the Harold Evans' style of photography. Their bible was his book *Pictures On A Page*. He demonstrated how effective layout and presentation could become with the creative use of photographs. I wanted their commitment by promising them more space than they ever had before, a closer relationship with the writers and, because of the lack of union demarcation lines, the ability to develop and print their own pictures. Beyond that lay not a new philosophy but something that a newspaper executive had seldom told his news photographers before: ' Go for the image behind the occasion. Do not think in conventional terms by getting the subject right in front of the lens. Stand back a bit and try to see the event from a different perspective.' It went against current thinking and practice. The usual procedure of getting photographs was for a 'rat pack' of Fleet Street photographers to descend on one event and all jostle for position in a highly unseemly way and then be surprised that they all ended up with very similar photographs.

The other part of the philosophy and practice of the picture desk was more simple. Because of budget restrictions, I was only able to offer staff jobs to three people thus severely limiting the number of photographic assignments that could be covered in one day. To that end, knowing that we could not compete on equal terms with other newspapers, we decided not to cover the type of jobs everyone else was. These ideas consolidated during the dummy period and as a result, the photographic standards of *The Independent* are remarkably high. In those days we decided to place not necessarily the best news photograph on the front page, but the best photograph of the day. We assumed that newspaper readers were tired of seeing endless photographs of Mrs Thatcher or the Princess of Wales on the front page and events were to prove us right.

One advantage we had over other newspapers then was a Nikon wire machine which enabled us to send photographs down a telephone line. It was another example of using new technology to improve the operation of a newspaper. Until then normal practice in Fleet Street, because of union restrictions, had been to send two NGA men to, say, a political party conference, one to develop the films given to him by a photographer and another to transmit them from a wire machine to the wire room at head office, where another NGA man took the print off and eventually handed it to the picture editor. During this dummy period we used it to transmit photographs from the party conferences straight to our wire machines on the picture desk. It took less than two minutes to send a photograph that way. Since then the wire transmitter has been to Reykjavik for the Gorbachev/Reagan summit, to Zeebrugge for the ferry disaster, to European football matches and up and down Britain. Other newspapers are now using them extensively.

The printed dummies which began on 2 September continued. It was a bizarre experience. Each day was like a normal working day on a newspaper. We were working to deadlines, reporters were chasing stories, photographers were chasing pictures, but the paper was not on sale anywhere. News reporters had to trot out a smart opening line every time they rang up people for a quote for an article: 'This is *The Independent*. We are a new newspaper and we won't be coming out until 7 October but can I interview you for tonight's newspaper.' They received some rude replies.

It was equally strange having spent the previous day and half the night working on a live newspaper to see no signs of it on the newsstands on the way to work the following morning.

Every day we continued to learn a little bit more about the computer systems and our own abilities. It was an amazing piece of luck that so many people in various departments had worked together on *The Times* or *Sunday Times*. This provided a natural homogeneity which smoothed out the day's production. It meant that journalists who knew each other could speak in a sort of shorthand at a close level.

As 7 October, the big day, loomed ever closer, there was a general air of ordered stress. The pressure was immense and AWS kept on saying that the launch could still be postponed at the last minute if everything was not in place and working smoothly.

On 5 September, he sent the following memo to all editorial staff:

Launch timetable

I see the period until launch being used as follows:

Monday, 8 September. No dummy. Post mortem. I would like to meet separately with home and foreign in the morning, other departments in the afternoon. At six o'clock there will be a budget meeting for heads of department.

Tuesday, 9 September to Friday, 12 September. Dummies printed in Portsmouth. No market research. The priority will be to prove that we can meet all the page deadlines.

No Sunday working.

Monday, 15 September. No dummy. De-briefing on first week's market research, 10 am to 12.30pm.

Tuesday, 16 September to 18 September. Dummies printed at one of our printers. No market research.

Friday, 19 September to Thursday, 25 September. Second period of market research with printed copies.

Sunday working for the Monday paper.

Friday, 26 September. No dummy. Post mortem.

Sunday, 28 September to Sunday, 5 October. Printed dummies. Simultaneous running of all printing plants. Full test of distribution systems.

Monday, 6 October. Launch issue.

The die was cast and the pattern laid down. Nothing, it seemed, would stop us now. We were still crossing AWS's 1,000 bridges; we probably had about 50 to go. As people became more aware of the keyboards and the capabilities of the layout system, the production and gathering of news stories and the output of pages grew in pace.

As part of the ordered plan, the ten so-called GT68 layout operators had had an intensive training course which began on 7 July and carried through until the start of the printed dummies. This was a whole new skill. Instead of drawing layouts on paper and then giving those to a compositor to make-up either with hot metal or galleys of type, this method produced layouts on a screen. It was strangely intangible and most of the page editors working with the GT68 operators still drew their schemes on paper first.

The GT68 has a command which enables the operator to call up a completed page on screen and scroll it from the top of the page to the bottom. It was an active proof that the page did exist somewhere in the system and very useful as a last-minute check on the spelling of the headlines, or whether rules had been left out. It is virtually impossible to read individual lines of type but does act as a final check. This ability to see an entire page on screen was an electronic marvel to all in the office. When a page review was being done, most, if not all, people in a section would stop what they were doing to cluster around the screen on which their work was displayed. The Sports Department, not famous for quiet behaviour or a cloistered life, would let out whoops of enjoyment when their sports pages appeared on screen. Sometimes they clapped and applauded as though they were watching Bryan Robson score a goal for England. It was good-natured fun and acted as a safety valve for the build-up of tension.

During these frenetic but structured weeks, intensive promotion and market research was taking place, some of it based on the printed copies. In what was the biggest promotional mailshot ever conducted by a newspaper, three million leaflets about *The Independent* were delivered around Britain. The homes were picked as those in areas most likely to have the most number of potential *Independent* readers according to age and social class profile. The leaflet explained a lot about *The Independent's* profile with a letter from AWS which read in part: 'During more than 20 years in Fleet Street, I watched the deterioration in national newspapers. Appalling labour problems and corrosive management policies made progress a hopeless prospect. I became convinced it was necessary to start again. We prize even-handed reporting and good writing. Accuracy, clarity, wit – these are the qualities we ask of our journalists.'

The clever marketing ploy in the leaflet was asking people not to judge the new paper in one day but to take it for three weeks by placing an order with their newsagent. If at the end of that time they decided not to carry on buying it, their money would be refunded if they wrote a letter to the editor explaining why. In the end only one person claimed a refund but later refused to accept it.

The purpose of the dummies was to test our journalists, our technology, our printing and distribution systems and, not least, our potential readers. Copies of the dummies printed in Portsmouth were delivered to London and were available early in the morning to be taken by courier to a panel of 320 test readers in Bromley, Pinner, Barnet and Putney. All the readers were asked by Research Surveys of Great Britain Ltd to try the paper for a week and to treat *The Independent* as they would normally a daily newspaper of this type in order that as realistic a reaction as possible to the paper could be obtained.

They were asked to keep a daily diary and were then interviewed on the telephone for their immediate reactions. Later a detailed in-home interview was conducted. Some the main findings were:

* A fifth of the sample gave the paper a very favourable initial impression rating. This rose to 81 per cent when the fairly favourable responses were included. Immediate reactions to the general presentation and layout were extremely positive.

* Most readers thought that *The Independent* was interesting, enjoyable and easy to read.

* It was well rated on most aspects in comparison to their usual newspapers.

* More than half rated it at least a little bit better than their own usual paper.

* A significant minority (14 per cent) actually thought that the paper was much better than the one they usually took.

* Quality paper readers (*Times, Telegraph, Guardian*) found the length of news stories about right, but readers of the *Daily Mail* and the *Daily Express*, not surprisingly found them a little too long.

In more general editorial terms, extremely high ratings were given for the quality of the print and the clarity of the photographs. Readers thought that the arts news, TV pages and foreign news were covered better than their usual papers. One criticism, which was to remain, was that the paper lacked humour and could be more light-hearted. After the market research findings, more emphasis was given to Lifestyle and a clearer distinction made between City and Business stories.

There was some light relief throughout September and right up to launch with the Great Eagle Saga. Back in June, AWS had decided that the paper needed some sort of symbol next to the masthead. At first a skyline of London was produced but that was rejected as being too biased towards the south. Later on, in July, the eagle was suggested as a symbol of freedom. AWS concurred and the search began for the right eagle. Eagle-drawers from all over the country were involved. Many versions appeared in the design department; some were wonderful examples of realistic art with every tail feather in place. Some would have worked very well on a printed book cover or frontispiece but were useless for newsprint. Some lost all definition when reduced to fit next to the title piece. Somehow, probably because eagle drawings were flying all over the place, word reached the newsroom where many hated the prospect. It was the start of the 'kill the chicken' campaign that was to rage furiously for weeks ahead. However, AWS would not budge and retreated to his eyrie to await further developments.

When AWS realised that a finely drawn eagle was impractical for our purposes, he said to me: 'Get me an eagle that is crude but effective. Strong and dynamic. Even a bit naff.' As ever, time was running short and I decided to ask Geoff Adams, a freelance graphic artist who was doing a day's work for me, to have a go. He proved the ideal choice and three hours later an eagle fluttered onto my desk. I had it enlarged and reduced and it still remained crude but effective. Triumphantly I marched in to see AWS. *The Independent* eagle was born and has remained on the front page ever since. Copies of it leaked into the newsroom. The office took sides – roughly half wanted to strangle the chicken in its infancy before the launch issue, the other half saw it as a strong symbol of our identity. Reports appeared in other newspapers and magazines.

Still AWS would not waver. On 7 October the eagle landed on doormats all over Britain. It was here to stay. It is used on our letterheads, visiting cards and a wide range of promotional material from full-size posters to marketing display stands. It has become a logo or trademark for *The Independent* in a way no-one dreamed possible.

The dummies continued and the experiments went on. We decided to try colour photographs. On Saturday, 6 September a photograph taken by David Ashdown of Ginny Leng riding at the Burghley Three-Day Event appeared on the back page. The colour was not good and some hopes for the strong use of colour evaporated. We tried again on Friday, 26 September with another Ashdown picture of Monty Spindler, a boardsailer. The results were better but still not as good as we had hoped.

There was indecision over where to place the summary or index box on page one and which type to use. It was an important decision because it affected the entire appearance of the front page and determined the use of photographs and main headlines. I have counted six variations in type and position between 2 September and launch day. The summary, which had been one of the original design requirements, began in fact as an index, called 'Inside' in the printed dummy on 2 September and occupying column eight on top of the advertisement. It was broken up into subject headings with items for Features, Business, City etc with a few words about the main stories in those sections. Underneath it came an index box of the individual pages. It was strong and graphic but really nothing more than an extended index. On 11 September it changed again to be called 'News Summary', still in column eight but with paragraphs rather than headings referring to stories inside. By 18 September the title was changed back to 'Inside'. The typography of the headline changed three times more in the week of 22 to 26 September. On Thursday, 25 September it moved down to the bottom half of the page in column 1. I think my argument at the time was that the design of the front page was restricted by having it always in column eight. On Friday, 26 September, it was back up in column eight. On Wednesday, 1 October (Launch Day minus

Various eagles which were put forward for the masthead.

six) it was down below the fold of page one again; the following day, Thursday, 2 October it was back up in column eight again.

It stayed there and appeared on Launch Day inside a shadow box with yet another different headline and below the fold was a Summary box. The style was also a return to indexing lines with pictures and drawings to illustrate the stories mentioned. Stylistically it was brash and more in keeping with the editorial advertising slogans found on the front pages of some of the Sunday newspapers. It was to stay in that shape and form until Saturday, 10 January 1987. Later it changed to Summary and was just that – a compilation of the various stories on the pages inside.

There were many other cases of deciding where to place editorial features. Until the dummy issue of Thursday, 18 September, the Letters to the Editor occupied the last two columns of the Leader Page. The Diary was in column one of the facing page, known as the Oped (or opposite editorial) page. On the Thursday, the Diary moved to the Leader Page and the Letters to the first two columns of the Oped Page. The leading articles or editorials ran from the top to the bottom of columns 1 and 2. Later we conducted several design changes on the Leader Page spread.

At that stage the daily Book Review which was to remain an important innovation of *The Independent* was resting at the foot of the Arts Page. By the end of that week the book review had found a home at the foot of the Oped Page; it later moved to the Leader Page when the daily diary column was dropped and has remained there since.

I was still refining the livery of the pages , i.e. the page numbers, titles of the sections and the dateline. The point size of the page numerals went up and down from 10pts to 20pts. The section headings varied in typography from Century Roman to Century Bold to Franklin Gothic Condensed and back again. Although one can do endless designs on paper in an inactive way, such vital decisions as the livery which opens the page to the reader can only really be taken after seeing the various options in print.

On 18 September it appeared consistently through the paper in its present form. At that stage it was difficult to keep all departments fully aware of the design changes. The printed dummies would often have inconsistent styles, not through any attempts at departmental self-rule, but because the right design decisions had not been taken or the right formats written. The panel of readers must have been impressed by this amount of experimentation. Little did they know the truth.

The waiting and the experimentation was nearly over. The months of planning, the weeks of dummy runs had taken their toll of people. There were tired yet happy faces around the office. The journalists as always had been kept very well-informed about the progress of virtually everything. They were immediately aware of computer or systems faults because their output was so intimately linked to the electronic brain lurking on the ground floor.

News of any problems faced by the four printing plants were

The build-up to launch: The bottom one was the final choice.

relayed around the office. Democracy ruled. We heard about the distribution prospects. AWS and his founders had decided against setting up an independent system. Instead it was announced towards the end of September that *The Independent* had appointed W.H.Smith and British Rail as joint distributors using a combined road and rail network. The advertising staff under the able leadership of Adrian O'Neill were, as ever, very confident about their prospects for display advertising both for launch and the weeks ahead. Throughout September advertising agencies had been visiting 40 City Road and inspecting the dummies.

In the week before launch a £3 million press, poster, radio and TV advertising campaign began. There were 48 giant billboard sites, 10- and 40-second television commercials, 50- and 60-second radio commercials and full-page advertisements in the national press. The slogan that was to become an advertising classic was launched: 'It is. Are you?'. It was designed as a tease for that most loyal group of people, the ABC1 readers. O'Neill said: 'All our research has shown that our independence is a very important factor so we are going to be single-minded and make sure people know that we are financially independent, intellectually independent, editorially independent and politically independent.' A launch budget for the first 15 months had been put at £5 million. This included the supply of point-of-sale material – stickers, posters etc – to the 42,000 newsagents in Britain.

Everyone took the dummy runs very seriously. Although they were not on sale to the public – in fact strict security took place to ensure that even the journalists' copies did not leave the building – it was for real. There were heated arguments about the quality of this article or the success of that graphic. Open debate was expected. Journalists freely criticised journalists in other departments knowing that they could expect the same in return. The atmosphere was very different to the insularity of departments at *The Times* or *The Daily Telegraph*.

AWS finally decided that he wanted centred headlines and by-lines. The change was made in time for launch. Formats were being written up to the last minute and rewritten in the weeks after launch as problems arose.

The great train was nearing the end of its 1,000 bridges. It could still plunge into the ravine of lost opportunities from any one of them. A power cut that knocked out the computer system on 18 September and left the building in darkness for many hours just when the shareholders came round to see what progress had been achieved, made us realise how fate could always play a part in the best-laid plans. A back-up emergency generator was immediately ordered.

There was no dummy produced on Monday, 6 October. Final changes were being made. Some exclusive stories that had been polished and honed to perfection were waiting in the computer's memory bank to appear on the nation's newsstands and Britain's breakfast tables.

The eagle had taken off and was circling over 40 City Road, getting ready to land. There were to be no more chances to change our minds. Anyway it wasn't really going to be Issue No 1, after all those dummies it would just be Issue 30.

Chanel's fitted Spencer jacket and bell skirt in black wool crêpe at Paris
Haute Couture in January 1988. (Photo: Suresh Karadia)

9: The Launch

Ah, but a man's reach should exceed his grasp,
Or what's a heaven for?

Robert Browning (1812–1889)

It was, they said afterwards – the media pundits, the circulation experts, the marketing men – the most successful launch of a new publication. For many journalists at 40 City Road, Monday, 6 October was an anti-climax; for others it was the most exciting day of their professional lives. By then journalists had a well-defined trust in the ability of Steve Conaway, Chris Hugh-Jones and their computer staff to cope with system problems. What were remote and unfathomable, and remain so, were the printing plants and distribution networks. Most journalists were used to seeing their newspaper roll off the presses in the same building as they worked in. They had grown accustomed to giant lorries, laden with rolls of newsprint, arriving outside their offices, and lorries and vans leaving hours later with the printed product.

They were never to see the same at *The Independent*. The pages departed down a phone line to the printing works and that was the last they saw of them until the first copies arrived back in the office after midnight from the nearest plant, then at Sittingbourne, Kent. And today of all days they would have to wait until then to see the first real issue.

The day began. Some people arrived earlier than usual to sit at their desks and turn on the VDTs, with just a faintly irrational fear that perhaps the gremlins had been at work again and that that carefully-filed story might have mysteriously disappeared overnight. Some of the tensions began to abate as journalists and staff all over the building settled into the routine they had adopted during the last few weeks.

Others made joking but nervous comments: 'This is it. This is the big one. Let's get it right tonight.' A chorus of 'Here we go, here we go, here we go' – the rallying cry of thousands of football fans up and down Britain – rolled up the office from the Sports Department, as usual full of high spirits and high jinks.

As had been the pattern for several days, the TV camera crews and radio interviewers began to arrive soon after 9.30 am. Linda Tanner tried hard to organise them as they began to run their cables around the office and to dazzle people with their powerful lights. Journalists had become blasé about the constant media attention the new paper was receiving. It was all good publicity and, so much the better that *The Independent* itself was news. That kind of exposure and advertising would cost a fortune to buy. The only interest was to see which one of the 'star journalists' was going to be interviewed next.

The morning editorial conference was unusually well-attended. The TV cameras were waiting to capture the great occasion. There was some unseemly jostling for places within camera range as AWS told the TV men that they only had a certain number of minutes before they would have to leave. The lists of possible stories were read out by the various departmental editors. Everyone listened intently as the temperature rose in the stuffy conference room – later known as the Wendy House – from the presence of the TV lights and so many eager participants in this day of reckoning.

In every technical area possible, the right plans had been laid and executed. The mechanical structure of the paper was installed and working – yet there was always one area which could not be pre-planned – news. AWS had said the previous week: 'What we need now is a really good story, like Westland [a reference to the row over the Westland helicopter company which fell into financial difficulties and caused the resignation of two Government ministers]. We need something which we can take by the scruff of the neck and show that we can run with it faster and better than the rest.' The newspaper needed a chance to demonstrate the talents of its reporters, the skills of its sub-editors, the efficiency of its computerised typesetting and layout and the speed of its distribution. As the conference progressed it emerged that there was nothing startling enough at that early stage in the morning to give the journalists much confidence in producing a dramatic front page. Perhaps this was AWS's X-factor – the unforeseen problem that may occur even when all the best planning has been done.

As professionals, the journalists knew that as the day wore on 'things were bound to pick up'. If they didn't, it would take all their skills to produce a newspaper that firmly announced its arrival on the newsstands.

At the end of the main editorial conference, there is usually a less well-attended discussion about which leading articles or editorials to run that day. It was suggested that there should be an editorial announcing the arrival of the newspaper. AWS was against this. His usual practice is to urge journalists to avoid undue self-regard but not publicity if it is in the interest of the newspaper. Later that day he did write an article or statement of intent which appeared in column eight of page 2 (see below).

As the day progressed, writers and sub-editors began producing the early pages of the newspaper – the listings pages, the health page, the arts page. On the photographic side how could we repeat the successes of the early dummies? Brian Harris came on the telephone from Bournemouth where the Conservative Party Conference was to start the following day. He said he had a wonderful picture of a policeman standing on a roof clutching a high-powered automatic rifle. It sounded ideal in the light of the massive security

The first issue: Everything is in place and the final design carried out by in-house staff.

'Missile tube blast sank Soviet sub'

By Mark Urban
Defence Correspondent

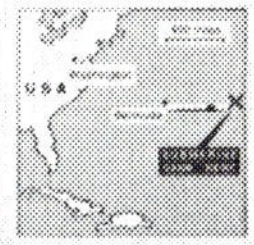

SUBMARINE design experts said last night that an explosion in a missile launch tube caused the damage which sank the stricken Soviet Yankee class submarine in the Atlantic Ocean.

According to one, the force of the blast — caused by missile fuel rather than warheads — was such that it would have blown off access hatches, and may well have "split the whole tube".

The Yankee-I class submarine carries 16 SS-N-6 ballistic missiles. The tubes in which they are held are extremely strong, being designed to cope with the forces involved in launching missiles under water. At least one of the liquid-fuelled missiles exploded, following a fire during manoeuvres.

This allowed water to rush into the rest of the submarine. It is not known whether the explosion happened before or after the submarine surfaced on Saturday night.

After it surfaced the crew were able to assess the damage, which included a gaping hole, where the missile tube hatch had blown off.

Soviet merchant ships took most of the 120-strong crew off the boat. Some sailors stayed on board, trying to cut back the listing over the missile section so that they could patch the hole.

The merchantman Krosnogyardeisk took the submarine in tow on Sunday. The Pentagon believed the boat was out of danger because the Yankee class have great inbuilt buoyancy — all 16 launch tubes can be full of water without affecting seakeeping qualities.

But the blast was so strong that it weakened the whole missile section, which flooded in heavy seas during yesterday morning. The submarine sank to three miles of water — too deep for the boat's lifeboats to withstand the pressure. They would have "popped" as the boat sank.

The compartment housing the Yankee's two nuclear propulsion reactors is the strongest part of the boat and would have been the last section to collapse — the rest of the hull could have imploded first.

The wreck lies so deep that salvage by any current methods would be difficult, if not impossible.

Scientists do not believe that there is any environmental risk from either the reactors — if they have broken up — or the missiles. According to Professor John Fremlin, a British specialist in radioactivity, it would take 1,000 years for any contamination to reach the surface.

At least three Soviet submarines have been lost at sea in recent years despite a major effort by Soviet designers to make them safer, more efficient and more comfortable to work in.

The Yankees are by no means old by Soviet standards. They are of a similar layout and design for Britain's Polaris boats. Nineteen Yankee-Is were built at the Severodvinsk 402 and Komsomolsk-na-Amur yards between 1967 and 1975. Soviet nuclear powered boats are anything up to 28 years old.

Lifecrafts sighted, page 8

Conservatives try to halt sterling slide

By Sarah Hogg and Andrew Marr

THERE WILL be no pre-election spending spree, Norman Tebbit, the Conservative Party chairman, promised yesterday.

Questioned about the intense pressure on the pound, Mr Tebbit predicted that the Conservative conference, which begins this morning in Bournemouth, would have a steadying influence on the market.

Meanwhile, it became known that the president of the German central bank has been called in for special consultations by Mrs Thatcher. This is strong evidence that the Prime Minister is actively reconsidering membership of the mechanism of linked exchange rates within the European Monetary System.

The Bundesbank, which yesterday confirmed the London visit by Mr Pöhl, supported sterling by publicly intervening in the currency markets, after pressure from the British at the Washington meetings of finance ministers last week.

Since then the British Government has struggled to resist a rise in interest rates, but the pound has continued to fall against the mark, closing in London yesterday below DM2.87. The bank of England's sterling index against all major currencies dropped to 66.9, and would have fallen further if the dollar had not also been weak.

The Prime Minister has continued to insist that "the time is not ripe" for Britain to risk starting up the mark by joining the exchange rate mechanism of the EMS. However, her secret invitation to Mr Pöhl suggests a new realisation that the EMS offers the only possible haven for a weak pound.

In Bournemouth yesterday, Mr Tebbit said: "It will be absolutely plain that we are not going on a pre-election spending spree, that we are sticking to our financial targets in Government."

He also said that growing evidence that the Opposition parties were in decline, "and that we are well set on the way to being returned again at the next election and I think those two things together will probably exercise a tremendous steadying influence and my move some of the uncertainty that has been besetting sterling recently," he said.

Asked whether an interest rate rise would not immediately follow the Conservative conference, Mr Tebbit said the steadying factors would remain through the rest of the year, though he was making no promises.

He said: "I don't make promises about interest rates and put down the Chancellor, but as you know we've had these suggestions about higher interest rates before and they have fizzled out."

Mr Tebbit said there would be no wrapping promises to meet concern about the National Health Service, education and unemployment. A good general did more than generalise, he said in an article for the party's newspaper, *Conservative Newsline*.

"We will begin to set out what we pass to achieve. There will be specific targets in each area, and we will say by when we aim to reach them," he said.

Yesterday David Owen urged the Government to join the European Monetary System before the end of this week, arguing that the core was "overwhelming", and that "the Government should act try and set out the Conservative Party Conference before doing so".

"It would be far preferable if the under-the-counter deal with the Bundesbank were made explicit and open," Dr Owen said. Dr Owen claimed that it was "almost uniquely unfavourable" notes "the Bundesbank intervenes, and the UK alone pays the bill." However, the Bank of England yesterday confirmed that the currencies are supported also boost to repay the costs of intervention.

Outlook: Page 19

An armed policeman keeping watch yesterday from the roof of the Bournemouth centre where the Conservative Party Conference opens today. *Conference security, Page 2*

Terrorist 'helped by Syrian envoy'

By Heather Mills
Courts Correspondent

SYRIAN INTELLIGENCE instructed an alleged Arab terrorist to sacrifice his pregnant girlfriend in a time-bomb blast on an El Al jumbo jet at 39,000 feet, the Old Bailey heard yesterday.

"It was one of the most callous acts of all time," said Mr Roy Amlot, prosecuting.

When the bomb plot failed, it was claimed Syrian diplomats, led by the Ambassador to Britain, became involved in an attempt to help the Arab escape.

The jury was told Nezar Hindawi, 32, calmly kissed good-bye his Irish lover, Ann Murphy — five and a half months pregnant — as she was about to board a plane at Heathrow Airport, after concealing three pounds of high explosives and a detonator hidden in a pocket calculator in her baggage. He had promised to meet her off the jet in Tel Aviv so the pair could be married in four days.

But for the "most impressive alertness" of Israeli airline security staff who discovered the bomb, 32-year-old Miss Murphy and her unborn child would have perished in the mid-air blast along with the 358 other passengers and 17 crew members, said Mr Amlot.

"Miss Murphy was no suicidal terrorist bomber. She was a simple, single Irish girl. Hindawi used her innocence to try and get the bomb on the aircraft," he said.

Hindawi, a Jordanian journalist of no fixed address, denies attempting to blow up flight 016 from New York via Heathrow to Tel Aviv on 17 April this year, and possessing a gun and ammunition. But in an interview with police, read to the court by Mr Amlot, Hindawi claimed he had been recruited by Syria "to attack Israeli targets in return for money".

He said he had been hired in Damascus by a Baathism Said, the head of Syrian Air Force intelligence.

Mr Amlot said Hindawi claimed Syrian Arab airlines were responsible for bringing in to the United Kingdom explosives, drugs and guns, and that Syria security officers were instructed in air crews.

He claimed he was instructed by Said to blow up the El Al jet and to "use a girl because it is more secure that way". He claimed he was given the bomb at the Royal Garden Hotel, Kensington, used as a stop over by Syrian air crews.

Hindawi told police that when the bomb was discovered he was given a letter, told to go to the Syrian Embassy and to hand it to the Syrian Ambassador in person.

He said he was greeted warmly by the Ambassador, who called Damascus for instructions. He was then taken to a house in West Kensington where his hair was cut and dyed.

But the next morning when two men tried to take him back to the Embassy, "he took fright and ran off," said Mr Amlot. He went to the London Visitors Hotel in Ruislip Park where he was later arrested.

Hindawi's former girlfriend, Dublin-born Miss Murphy, broke down as she told the court she had no idea a bomb had been planted in her luggage until police with dogs arrived at the El Al checkout where she was being searched and questioned.

In a barely audible voice and looking pale and thin, Miss Murphy told the court she and Hindawi became lovers during a two year on-off relationship, when he would disappear for months at a time, never saying where he was going.

She had twice become pregnant by him — the first pregnancy ended in a miscarriage.

She told the jury of seven men and five women that she was five months pregnant when Hindawi suddenly arrived on her doorstep after one of his long absences.

He told her he loved her and wanted to marry her and to take her on holiday to Israel.

He could not accompany her on the flight as he was already booked onto another. But he gave her a buy to take on the plane and helped her pack.

She told the jury that in the taxi they shared to the airport he placed batteries in a pocket calculator and then packed it in her bag. "He seemed very nervous but I did not take heed of it," she said.

At the airport on the way to the check-in, "he kissed me on both cheeks and left me. He said he was going to another terminal to take another flight and I believed him," she said. Miss Murphy told the court Hindawi once asked her if she knew anyone in the IRA but I said I didn't know anyone.

The hearing was adjourned until today.

Heseltine challenges Government over jobs

By Anthony Bevins
Political Editor

A DIRECT challenge to the Government's industrial and unemployment strategies has been launched by Michael Heseltine on the eve of the Conservative Party conference.

In an interview with *The Independent*, the former Secretary of State for Defence revealed that he would run for the leadership after Margaret Thatcher retires, but he has rejected colleagues' requests that he should challenge her quickly. And he should challenge the Prime Minister to a leadership contest when the Commons returns next month.

Mr Heseltine believes Mrs Thatcher will win the next election with a heavily-reduced overall majority of between 30 and 40 seats, but he has strongly condemned the absence of a Conservative policy to attack the problem of unemployment in the inner-city "stress areas".

In his own outline manifesto, which is designed to take the Conservative Party back into the centreground of British politics, Mr Heseltine wants £8bn of mortgage and pension subsidies to be shifted towards wealth-creating investment.

He also wants the Treasury, "an anachronism", to be cut down in size and the Department of Trade and Industry to be given the lead role in working together the interests of shareholders, managers and workers.

With the Conservatives gearing up for an education debate in Bournemouth this afternoon, he said that it should not be "beyond the wit" of the Government to re-invest £700m savings, created by falling rolls and a reduction in the number of educational establishments into the surviving schools.

Asked whether he would be an eventual contender for party leadership, Mr Heseltine said: "Oh Lord, I would be as interested — as in the leadership of the Conservative Party as virtually every other member of the Cabinet. I have never seen any purpose in pretending one is less ambitious than one knows all one's colleagues to be."

Interview, page 17

Pope's homage to obscure saint

From Patrick Marnham
in Curé d'Ars

THE POPE chose to spend the whole of the third day of his pilgrimage to France in one village, formerly the parish of the Curé d'Ars.

While the Pontiff was in Ars a last impossible for almost anyone else to go there. Even the villagers were obliged to display identity cards and were prevented from walking freely around their own village. I saw one old lady being forbidden by a captain of the Gendarmerie Nationale from entering the house where she had been born.

Ars has been a place of special importance for the Pope since he was a young priest. Indeed, the example of Saint Jean-Marie Vianney, the Curé d'Ars, means more to the Polish pope than it does to many French priests.

The curé was a humble man who was appointed to this particular parish in 1818. He experienced as a contrast spread slowly throughout France. Pilgrimages to this little village grew, and for the last six years of his life the cure was literally a prisoner of this followers. He died in 1859, was canonised in 1925 and declared to be the patron saint of all parish priests.

Since the Second World War his cult has dwindled. Ars remains a little village bypassed by the main roads, not a great pilgrimage centre. When it was first announced that the Pope had decided on coming, some French priests were protested at being reminded of the example of this uncharitable zeal, a priest who spent his life either seated in the confessional or on his knees.

Yesterday, in a vast marquee erected in a meadow outside the village, the Pope reminded all the bishops and many of the 6,000 priests and seminarians of the importance of their forgotten saint.

Like so many of his sermons, it was highly political, but couched in code. He referred to the perils facing the church due to the lack of vocations, but insisted that priestly functions were unique and could never be delegated to lay people. In saying this he was denying the possibility of such innovations as a married priesthood.

When he referred to the hours spent in prayer by the Curé d'Ars, he was admonishing those priests who concentrate their efforts on social work. He urged the priests of France to return to their parishes and address themselves to the sins of their parishioners, to re-store a stricter observance of Sunday, and to insist on private confessions.

operation to pre-empt another IRA bombing outrage and 'a definite candidate' for the front page. He described the shape to me as being vertical. I told Nigel Lloyd who would be producing the front page. He seemed unimpressed and rightly wanted to see what else would come in.

The second editorial conference of the day was held at 6.15 pm and the final decisions were taken about which stories were going to be placed on the front page or on inside pages. The armed policeman was the best offering for our main picture. There was a good foreign story by Mark Urban, Defence Correspondent, about why a Soviet Yankee-class submarine sank in the Atlantic Ocean; a graphic map showing the location was organised to go with it. Colin Hughes, Political Correspondent, came up with an exclusive story about plans to create between 10 and 12 city technical colleges. Heather Mills, Courts Correspondent, wrote a report on a case involving a Syrian terrorist. Anthony Bevins, Political Editor, produced an exclusive interview with Mr Michael Heseltine, the former Defence Minister. The front page basement position was occupied by a charming tale from Patrick Marnham, Paris Correspondent, about the Pope's visit to Ars to pay homage to Saint Jean-Marie Vianney, the Curé d'Ars, and patron saint of all parish priests. Colin Wheeler provided a lighter, more satirical touch with a pocket cartoon about Luton Football Club.

The honours for the main story, or splash, were jointly shared by Sarah Hogg, Business and Finance Editor, and Andrew Marr, Political Correspondent, with another exclusive story about Mrs Thatcher planning to meet the head of the German Bundesbank in a effort to halt the decline in sterling. It was all sound and interesting material but not instantly attention-grabbing. Above them all, *The Independent* eagle hovered, about to land, clutching the first edition in its talons.

The evening wore on. Everything was working smoothly. There appeared to be no problems with the computer systems or with the pages being faxed to the printing plants. Against the constant background hum of the VDTs and the photographic wire machines could be heard the occasional pop of a champagne cork as people, having completed their part in the night's operation began to celebrate. In other departments whisky was produced and poured into paper cups. AWS was moving around the office gently inquiring if everything was going according to plan. Televisions around the office were switched on for journalists to watch themselves making the news.

The front page was the last page to be finished on screen – normal practice. It was a few minutes late but nothing serious. It was sent to the typesetters at 9.35pm and appeared as a bromide page, all complete apart from the picture, graphic and advertisement, 25 minutes later. Anxious executives gathered around it in the computer room, trying to spot mistakes. It was then faxed with the back sports page to the four printing plants. Bridge 990 had been safely crossed. The editor's office resembled a florist's shop by then, with garlands and bouquets from well-wishers. Celebratory cake was being handed out to all who entered.

On the floor above, a large room next to the cuttings library had been cleared for the party. Melanie Ward, PA to the Editor and Deputy Editor and a powerhouse of organisational ability, had laid on waiters and what seemed like one year's produce of an entire Champagne vineyard (in fact she had ordered 28 cases or 336 bottles). The celebrations and the waiting began.

Everyone seemed exhausted yet exhilarated. It was as though we were all new parents. We had been through a long pregnancy, a smooth labour, a trouble-free birth and we were just waiting for the baby to come back from the post-delivery room. The champagne flowed and flowed and flowed. In the end the desperate waiters gave up trying to pour individual glasses and started handing out full bottles.

AWS arrived later and was greeted like a movie star. The throng of merry-makers threatened to engulf him and 'press the flesh' with a hundred handshakes. At 12.30 am the first copies of the newspaper arrived in the office from Sittingbourne. Everyone who could grabbed a copy – the first real for-sale issue. It was an emotional and proud moment. The doubters had been put to flight and the end of the line was in sight, there were only a few more bridges to cross. AWS could resist the calls for a speech no longer.

Characteristically, it was brief and to the point. The ending was drowned in applause: 'Thanks to so many people for so much . . .' A chorus of 'For he's a jolly good fellow' resounded around the room and the partying continued. Several people went up to AWS and asked him to sign their copies. He obliged between the popping flashlights of the photographers. Towards 3am the party broke up and dishevelled revellers drifted off home. The day was won.

The collective hangover of the following day was relieved as favourable reports about the printing and distribution of the first issue began to filter back into the office. It was a sellout. More than 650,000 copies were printed and sold. There was a slight technical hitch over one colour page at Sittingbourne. That apart, it was a model launch.

It was only then that most of us sat down to read the statement on page 2 by AWS. It is worth repeating here:

'The question most often asked in the days preceding the launch of *The Independent* has been: what makes it different; why should people change from their existing newspapers to read it?

'We have deliberately eschewed difference for its own sake, for example by resisting the temptation of being the first quality tabloid or by over-using editorial colour. Our intention is to be within the best traditions of British quality newspapers, but at the same time to be classic with a twist.

'Above all, *The Independent* exists because of a shared belief on the part of its investors and the people who work for it that the readers of quality newspapers are not well-served and that journalism of the highest standard cannot easily flourish when impeded by union restrictive practices or by the political prejudices of the typical newspaper proprietor.

'The ownership of *The Independent* is spread between more than 30 financial institutions and its own employees. No investor holds more than a 10 per cent stake, which under the articles of the company is the maximum permitted amount. Our investors are politically neutral. As long as we provide a return on their investment, they will not seek to influence any aspect of our editorial judgement. We are free to make up our own mind on policy issues, to expose commercial skullduggery and to query the establishment – however broadly defined, whether of left or right. We will both praise and criticise without reference to a party line. Our campaigning will emerge from our rt-steve-usrting [a gremlin in the system struck at this point] rather than the other way round.

'Our political, intellectual and financial independence distinguish us from our rivals. But, beyond being the first newspaper to opt out of the Lobby system, these are qualities which will be developed over time. There are, however, differences and innovations which are more immediately apparent.

'First and most obvious, news stories in *The Independent* are somewhat longer than the norm. Most of us get our news headlines from television and radio. We will try to go further and use our expert team of specialist writers to analyse and explain. There is a thin line between comment and analysis and the former has no place in news columns. At the same time our readers are busy people. Every day, the front page will provide a summary of the main points of the news and every section of the newspaper will carry an 'in brief' box.

'The leader page article will express the personal opinion of the author. In addition to the normal ration of leisure and general interest articles, we will carry each week a section on health, media and the workplace. We will display a strong bias in favour of the consumer, tackling education from the point of view of parents and students, health from the point of view of patients.

'The readers of *The Independent* will be people who are more than averagely interested in the arts. We are devoting substantial space, including two pages of everyday entertainment listings, to an adventurous arts coverage.

'Our sports pages, while remaining loyal to the traditional sports, will reflect the fact that tastes change. Participation sports, racket games, American football, Grand Prix motor racing and sailing will be reported consistently and authoritatively. And because opinion and argument are an essential ingredient in the enjoyment of sport, our writers will be controversial, even infuriating.

'During the past month we have daily been producing fully printed dummy newspapers, bringing all these ingredients together, getting used to the technology and learning to work as a team. One vital element, has however, until today been missing –

our readers. Your relationship with us will finally determine what sort of newspaper we are.'

Most of those principles and practices had been in AWS's mind since March 1985. Little had changed from concept to launch. He and his journalists had stayed together on the same track with no deviation.

The day after launch, AWS was very keen to lift people again, saying it was not just one day, but every day thereafter that a special effort must be made. His weary troops rallied to the call and day after day from launch the paper improved and changed.

The plaudits and the plaints poured in. Dog snaps at dog who is trying to invade his territory:

Max Hastings, Editor of *The Daily Telegraph*, who sent a magnum of champagne for the launch party and a wreath the day after, was quoted as saying: 'It's a respectable, honourable, responsible, pretty dull newspaper. It lacks humour. It will survive. When it has its financial crisis, some rich sugar daddy will come along and rescue it.'

Peter Preston, Editor of *The Guardian*: 'For a new paper it's lacking in new ideas, it looks a bit like *The Times* of five years ago. They need to offer something absolutely different. This is absolutely the same.'

Charles Wilson, Editor of *The Times*: 'The paper lacks the natural spirit, character and personality of an established paper.'

Predictable reaction perhaps, and, as it turned out, substantially wrong. Reaction from marketing and advertising was more praiseworthy:

Bill Jones, Press Buying Director at Davidson Pearce, said: 'As an initial offering, it's outstanding. It has a spark to it that the other qualities don't have.' However he did strike a note of caution: 'I wish it the best of luck: but I have a horrible feeling it won't reach its circulation target.'

Robert Dodds, Media Director at BBDO(UK), said he thought it would do brilliantly. 'The layout is fabulous and it's a good easy read.'

Brian Jacobs, Media Director at Leo Burnett, said: ' The biggest compliment I can pay is that it didn't look like a first issue. The mono reproduction is very good and I think it was extremely sensible of them not to use colour in the first issue.'

Ron de Pear, Media Director at J. Walter Thompson: 'It's very crisp and clear in layout. But it is somewhat wordy and worthy and lacks excitement. It's on the heavy side.'

'Worthy but dull', 'lacks humour and excitement'. Those were the two favourite criticisms of its detractors. They were wide of the mark in their estimation of what *The Independent's* readers wanted. To most in the media, a launch of a new newspaper, magazine or television station, should be an occasion to be dazzled, startled by its visual originality, its written excellence. They want a kaleidoscope of images to shock them out of their cynical, seen-it-all-before attitude. In truth, *The Independent* was launched in a wave of media-induced publicity, not self-generated promulgation. They expected more colour, real and figurative. What they got was a more serious and intense treatment of news affairs.

However there was a quantity of humour and human interest that seems to have escaped them. On page 5, Oliver Gillie, Medical Editor, wrote a small appraisal of Sir Harry Platt, a former president of the Royal College of Surgeons, who was 100 that day. Sir Harry, Mr Gillie informs us, owed his longevity to heredity and still drank a glass of sherry every day.

On the following page, reporter Nicholas Schoon wrote an amusing piece about scientists at Bristol University who were trying to build a robot which could play snooker. It came complete with a cartoon by Michael Heath.

On page 9, nearly a column and a half of space was devoted to 'Around The World', a collection of funny or unusual stories compiled from the foreign wire agencies by Steve Crawshaw.

To round off the humour or off-beat interest in the news pages alone, James Fenton, poet, writer and the paper's Far East Correspondent, penned a bizarre and amusing article about taking a live goat as a gift to Muslim guerrillas on Mindanao Island in the Philippines. A cartoon by Nicholas Garland rounded it off.

Later Miles Kington was to leave *The Times* to write a daily humorous piece; the front page basement slot was reserved for off-beat and humorous stories; more use was made of Michael Heath and Colin Wheeler.

Staff recollections of the great day are varied:

Brian Harris, photographer: 'This was the night we had all been waiting for. I was asked to cover the Conservative Conference at Eastbourne. All day I walked around looking for the picture to convey the impression of the unbelievable security surrounding the Tory Conference. By 6.30 pm, Andreas had decided on one of my pictures for the front page showing a sinister police officer looking like a Dirty Harry extra. That evening, exhausted and unable to attend the official launch party, I watched TV in my hotel room with a decent bottle of Something Red.'

Brenda Beazley, now Mowlem, PA to the Foreign Editor: '6 October was an exciting day but not that different from the previous few weeks because of the dummies. On 7 October having had to recover from the night before was a total surprise. We had practised for everything but not accounted for the public. The phones started ringing! This threw me totally off balance.'

Brian Hutt, circulation manager: 'My memories of launch night and day were those of elation. We achieved full distribution. Throughout 7 October all the reports we were receiving were good. The paper had been well-received and most of the reps reported a sellout. Everything had gone off according to plan. I had my worries, naturally, but it was tremendous.'

Michael McGuinness, Deputy Art Editor: 'My memories were thinking – tomorrow we have to do it all again. The launch was just the first day, we would have to keep on doing it all again and again.

Even at the party the main thing on my mind was tomorrow. All we had achieved was the first day.'

Melanie Ward, former PA to the Editor: 'I was wearing the bleep and as a result I could not drink as I was organising film crews and the like. I remember sitting in AWS's room at about 1am while everyone else was enjoying themselves upstairs at the party while Andreas was being interviewed by Breakfast Television. My feelings later were: is that it? I felt that we had done it but that was not enough because we had to do it again for another 365 days. I was amazed as well. We had produced a newspaper but I knew that many things had occurred by the skin of our teeth.'

Outside reaction to appearance was predictably mixed. I have tried to trace how the design evolved into a form that illustrated the specifics of its journalism. By definition, with longer stories than the norm, the initial appearance may seem grey, which is often equated with being dull; the Century typeface did, on launch, have a faintly antique look to it; the body text in Dutch did have an establishment air about it. But on balance they helped to give new readers the impression that the newspaper knew what it was doing and had been around for some time. Some people, notably Nick Lloyd, Editor of the *Daily Express*, said that *The Independent* appeared to be upmarket of *The Times*. Few at the newspaper knew it at the time but that's partly where the market gap lay.

After the first day which was a sellout, *The Independent* sold more than 500,000 for several days. Strangely enough the other quality newspapers in those early days only seemed to have lost about 1 to 2 per cent. By then, of course, everyone at the newspaper knew that the newspaper needed to sell 375,000 copies a day to survive and make money. At the time AWS said : 'We need to take about 190,000 readers from *The Times*, *The Daily Telegraph* and *The Guardian* – or about 8% of their combined daily circulation of 2.3 million.

The 1,000th bridge had been crossed. The Rubicon lay behind and led by its eagle standard bearer, a legion of new journalism had entered the old republic.

Voting for the Irish elections in Inishmore on the Aran Islands in
February 1987. (Photo: Jeremy Nicholl)

10: The First Year and the Future

The newspaper is of necessity something of a monopoly, and its first duty is to shun the temptations of monopoly. Its primary office is the gathering of news. At the peril of its soul it must see that the supply is not tainted. Neither in what it gives, nor in what it does not give, nor in the mode of presentation, must the unclouded face of truth suffer wrong. Comment is free but facts are sacred.

C.P.Scott (1846–1932)

For an overwhelming majority of employees and readers of *The Independent*, the first year was one of continued interest in a product they believed in, consolidation of its basic principles and a lot of fun.

The informal consultations and debriefings for the staff by management which had already become a feature of the democratic nature of the newspaper continued in the months after launch. Inevitably after everything seemed in place and working according to targets, they became less frequent. Information was readily available from the advertising, marketing or circulation departments but it was not disseminated in as thorough a way as before. There was, and remained, a full meeting with all the journalists to discuss what had taken place at the monthly board meeting. Despite the stated and asked-for confidentiality of these debriefings, unavoidably, word leaked and reached the newspaper's rivals at times. These leaks probably caused them more concern than it did *The Independent* as the emerging picture of success became clearer as the year progressed.

The Independent was always going to be market researched and editorial-led, AWS had told his investors and his staff. It was, but naturally the pressure on market research began to diminish as soon as progress accelerated. By the end of November 1987, a 'readership satisfaction monitor' was being carried out on an irregular basis every other month or so.

A week after the launch, research was undertaken to examine the type of people reading the newspaper, their likes and dislikes of the paper and their reactions to a particular part of the paper. In all, 1,200 people of A and B social standing and 800 of social class C1 were screened to identify readers of one or more issues of *The Independent*. Telephone interviews were then carried out with all the people meeting this criteria.

The main findings were as follows:

1) As predicted, a lot of readers came from the three established rivals.

2) A liking was shown for the layout, news coverage, print quality and lack of reporting bias.

3) Foreign news, home news and the listings sections were all rated favourably in terms of providing good coverage.

4) Some respondents disliked the size, some its seriousness and a minority thought that the paper did not have a strong personality.

The watching process continued – *The Independent* watching its readers and the marketing and media pundits watching *The Independent*. By the middle of November 1986, special research realeased through JICNARS (Joint Industry Committee for National Readership Surveys) showed that although *The Independent* had already gained support from the quality newspaper readers, it was placed as the least-upmarket quality daily. Despite some initial reservations that the new paper lacked identity, the research carried out on 5, 6 and 7 November indicated that *The Independent* had probably settled down to a little over one million readers each day or a sale of about 330,000. The research showed that after *The Guardian*, *The Independent* had the youngest readership profile of any quality daily – 53 per cent aged between 15 and 44. Despite its relatively low profile rating, *The Independent* had 72 per cent from the ABC1 social class, much higher than the *Daily Mail* or the *Daily Express*.

At that stage two-thirds of the readership were men. Many journalists felt that these figures reflected both an operational bias against so-called women's interest articles and a concomitant lack of space given to them. From a marketing point of view it seemed simpler than that – there was a dearth of home-delivered *Independents*, only 12 per cent compared with 50 per cent for *The Daily Telegraph*, which reduced the chances of a woman in the target readership reading her husband's copy which he might buy on the way to work.

It was too early to count the launch as an unqualified success but, measured in terms of Eddie Shah's *Today*, it certainly was. Display advertising was holding up well but classified was falling behind targets – partly because of the difficulty in such a competitive market in finding trained salespeople. An average of one-and-a-half pages a day in the first few weeks was not enough.

At some of the editorial meetings there were murmurings about trying to run a competition, nothing as vulgar as a bingo game, but something to generate more sales. AWS firmly squashed these notions. He said that the newspaper could sell more by running exclusive news stories and getting itself talked about editorially on the television or radio. This view was to remain one of his central beliefs.

On the design front, there were few outside complaints but inside we still felt the job was incomplete. Bob James, group editorial development officer for Westminster Press, wrote in *Printing World* on 26 November 1986: '*The Independent* has made a remarkable début. Time will tell whether it can woo enough readers from those other newspapers in Quality Street but, typographically speaking at least, it is already holding its own. In many respects it is in the forefront, demonstrating that there's more to a good read than mere writing. The titlepiece is a winner, suggests independence... The wide page has the feel of the broadsheets of old, with good margins and still eight columns of reasonable width. *The Independent* wins perhaps its highest marks in display and offers an object lesson for all in choosing a headline face and sticking to it. Basically it's a perfect marriage between Century Bold and Century Expanded (not to be confused with Century Extended). Logos and labels are good, and here and there is a nice relieving touch in the use of that elegant Latin Roman. Graphics are first-rate (three cheers for the Apple Macintosh).'

But James had a justifiable complaint that stemmed from inexperience with the keyboards and lack of sub-editing time. He wrote: 'When you find a piece of newspaper setting where as many as six lines in seven end with a hyphen you know that something is wrong.' Modern computer typesetting systems automatically hyphenate and justify text when a writer or sub-editor has finished with it. But in a hurry, it is easy to leave it as defined by the computer. An experienced operator can override the justification any way he or she likes. Quality control still had a long way to go.

A design problem which had caused widespread disagreement concerned the labelling of the specialist feature pages, motoring, media, education, health, living, and workplace. It was natural and customary to announce a difference between the news sections and features with either a change in headline typography or in livery or top of the page signposting. Clear signposting is an essential design requirement. Originally we had had the word Features in a lighter version of the Home News heading in between two rules at the top of the page. This was not thought strong enough. I experimented with a bigger headline size from 12pt to 14pt to 18pt to 24pt. It still did not look right; eventually, about a week before launch, AWS thought it might be different and attractive to have illustrated logos surrounding the heading. Dennis Bishop, one of our artists, came to the rescue and drew them. His execution was fine but the inclusion of blackboards and classroom for the Education page heading just seemed trite after a while and on 13 November, they were dropped. In their place, I put a simple 1pt box surrounding the heading in 36pt Latin Roman which was positioned a little way down from the dateline.

13 November was also a significant date as we ran the first colour front page picture. Photographer Brian Harris had been dispatched to the House of Lords to capture the State Opening of Parliament. His photograph reflected the solemn air of pomp and pageantry and was imbued with the majestic and magisterial colours of red, purple and black relieved by the white of the ermine. It was used in colour because it added an extra dimension to the occasion. Although the event was televised, the colour picture gave the

Overleaf, the first Leader Page spread: Letters were across two columns as were the editorial columns. The Diary has an old-fashioned logo.

THE INDEPENDENT
45 CITY ROAD, LONDON EC1Y 2DB
(Tel no 253 1222, telex 9419611 INDPNT)

A decent man buries his son

FOR the Argentine father, Mr Isaias Giménez, there were two moments last Saturday which brought a painful personal journey to an end. The first was the burial on the Falklands of his son, Miguel Angel Giménez. The second, the moment when he saw for himself the peak of Blue Mountain where his son's plane crashed in 1982.

For the last four years, he has sought single mindedly, to discover exactly what happened to Miguel Angel. He has resisted with dignity the pressures on him to allow his quest, and those of the other families he represents, to become one more national grievance, an occasion for patriotic indignation against the British. It is entirely appropriate that the British Government has allowed him to become the first Argentine citizen to set foot in the Falklands since the war.

But, though Mr Giménez has been allowed to complete his personal rites, he returns to London with further requests to make of the British Government. He wishes the same privilege to be extended to other parents who have never seen their sons' graves. He also hopes that the British Government can find a way of identifying the unidentified dead and of helping those parents who wish, as he did, that their sons might be brought home for burial.

The British Government has stated no objection to the return of the bodies, but the project has foundered on the disposition of both Governments to treat the matter on a government to government level. The British will repatriate the bodies if the Argentine Government will agree. Argentina refuses to ask. The result is stalemate, since the Argentine Government is afraid that Argentina's highly vocal patriotic lobby will accuse it of conceding a millimetre of sovereignty. For them, the war dead are already interred on Argentine soil in the "Malvinas". To talk of "repatriation" is treason.

Mr Giménez, who treats it as a private matter, is to propose that the Red Cross be invited to unblock the diplomatic impasse by acting on behalf of the families for the "transfer" of the bodies. He hopes thus to avoid putting President Alfonsin on the spot and to give the families the consolation of burying their dead where they wish and mourning them as they choose.

President Alfonsin is a humane and reasonable man who opposed the war in 1982, when few of his fellow politicians dared to. He has manoeuvred with skill and courage in the very narrow margins that the clashing forces of Argentine political life impose on him. He is trying to create in Argentina a strong civilian state on which the kind of military regime which invaded the Falklands can never again impose its will. For that alone he deserves our support.

If the intercession of the Red Cross would allow him to permit the return of the bodies to Argentina, then this country should grasp the opportunity to demonstrate our humanity and help to grant the wishes of Mr Giménez and his friends. It says nothing about the future of the islands to insist that the dead, and their families, be treated decently.

Schools for scandal

EDUCATION will be top of the agenda when the Tory Party conference opens today, as it should be. The evidence that many parents who use state schools are deeply worried about the standards their children attain is overwhelming; so is the evidence that some of our industrial competitors, West Germany and Japan, are achieving higher standards. There is little support for the claim that standards have fallen compared with 20 years ago. There is plenty of evidence that they have not risen enough.

Those Tories (including the Prime Minister but, not, apparently, Mr Kenneth Baker, the Education Secretary) who believe that the solution is to extend something called parental choice, possibly through the introduction of vouchers, are evading the real issues.

The idea that parents can choose schools as if they were choosing motor cars or vegetables is false. A faulty car can be traded in; a greengrocer who sells rotten fruit will lose his custom the following day. Parents do not want to switch schools more than once during a child's primary or secondary career.

What most parents want is a good, local school with adequate books and equipment and well-qualified, enthusiastic teachers. For too many, no such school is available. There is no guarantee that vouchers or any other fancy device for extending parental choice would improve things. A genuine, free market choice implies elastic supply. It implies the possibility of expanding popular schools while leaving empty places in the unfavoured ones. But empty classrooms cost money, as the Audit Commission told the government in a report earlier this year. That money would be better spent on books — or on raising teachers' pay to prevent those with the most marketable skills, in such subjects as physics and maths, from leaving.

Choice between different types of school is possible. Choice, say, between single-sex and co-educational schools, between schools with a bias towards technical subjects and those that concentrate on the humanities. Mr Baker's scheme for sponsored, city technical schools, which he is expected to announce today, would be a small, symbolic, step towards such diversity. But, whatever its label, every school should be capable of providing children with a decent education. No child should be abandoned to a rotten education just because his or her parents have made the wrong choice.

Foul play society

WATERLOO may have been won on the playing fields of Eton, but the battle against British thuggery today is being lost on the football field, and, for goodness sake, on the golf course. At the weekend, Australian golfer Greg Norman, a man built not to give a XXXX for a bit of heckling, said after winning the Suntory title that he had not won a tournament, but a battle, so viciously was he abused by spectators. His treatment cannot be excused as nationalistic fervour. It is unsporting, and can pervert justice. Yet the authorities seem prepared to minimise violence associated with sport. Luton Football Club obeyed government urging to control hooligans. Now the Football League, which "deplores" hooliganism, has penalised Luton for a ban on away supporters. If the authorities want to control violence, they cannot excuse hooliganism as a consequence of sporting jingoism. That is not fair play, and it underestimates a wider social evil.

Time for the BBC gentlemen to hand over to the players

William Rees-Mogg, former Vice-Chairman of the BBC, on the challenge facing Duke Hussey as he becomes broadcasting's new grandee

On the afternoon of Saturday 8 November the establishment will be having a field day near Shepton Mallet. The new Chairman of the BBC, Mr Marmaduke Hussey, will be there. The old Chairman of the Arts Council will be there. The Chairman of Lonrho, Mr Edward du Cann, has been invited. So has the Deputy Chairman of the Conservative Party, Mr Jeffrey Archer. Also invited are some 5,000 other members of the Somerset County Cricket Club, and the world's press.

The meeting is to decide whether to fire the three great Somerset cricketers, Mr Viv Richards, the greatest batsman in the world and perhaps a future Commonwealth Prime Minister, Mr Joel Garner, a sweet natured man though a leading member of the West Indies squad of unplayable fast bowlers, and Mr Ian Botham, the greatest aggressive all-rounder in cricket history, the Siegfried of the wicket.

The alternative policy is to fire the County committee, together with Mr Roebuck, their captain, who, like Sir Geoffrey Howe, has a first in law from Cambridge.

I shall finally make up my mind after hearing the argument, but as Chairman of the Arts Council all my sympathies are on the side of the artists rather than the bureaucrats.

Mr Hussey will be able to reflect on some of the similarities between the affairs of Somerset cricket and those of the BBC, the corporation for which he had now taken on the ultimate responsibility. Both Somerset cricket and British Broadcasting engage intense loyalties and generate fierce passions. But there is more to it than that.

In the early 1920s, the constitution chosen for the BBC was strikingly similar to that of a cricket club, a form of organisation which the English establishment has always well understood.

Even the initials BBC were reassuringly reminiscent of those of the MCC. There was to be a committee. The committee would be amateur. They would be part time and their tenure of office would be brief. They would meet in the pavilion to dispose of the affairs of the Corporation.

The committee, known as the Board of Governors, would appoint a Captain, known as the Director-General. He would have no standing in law — he is not mentioned in the charter — but would be given plenary power on the field of play. He was to be professional in his attitudes, like the Captain of a ship, the editor of a newspaper or Douglas Jardine on the bodyline tour. He would report to the Board but would not belong to it.

This, or something like it, is a practical way of running a single newspaper, a small radio station — such as the BBC originally was — or of course a cricket club. It amounts to despotism tempered by dismissal. Even on a small scale it invites dispute between the immediate power of the captain and the ultimate power of the committee. As a way of running a large and complex organisation it is quite hopeless. The Government seems to have recognised this; Mr Hussey is no amateur Chairman, but a lifelong professional in the communications business.

The present structure of the BBC is however unsatisfactory, from everyone's point of view. The Governors, miserably underpaid, take responsibility for an organisation they have ceased to control. Responsibility without power, as Baldwin might have said, has been the prerogative of the eunuch throughout the ages.

They feel themselves to be under the influence of continual bureaucratic manipulation, and read in the newspapers of decisions taken in their name of which they often thoroughly disapprove. They are aware that there are whole systems of communication inside the Corporation to which they have no access. They issue policy instructions which are solemnly noted and as solemnly disregarded.

To be a Governor of the BBC is therefore a frustrating experience, mitigated for some by the fact that Governors can fall in love with the Corporation and believe thereafter that it can do no wrong.

The position of the Director-General is perhaps even less fortunate. He is conscious of the professional skills which have brought him to the head of his profession. He is answerable to a random group of amateurs, appointed by successive Home Secretaries for various reasons.

He is charged with total responsibility for the conduct of the BBC, in terms of its management, its development and its editorial product. He is Editor in Chief of two television networks, four radio networks, regional television, local radio, world broadcasting in countless languages. He is chief executive of a business employing nearly 30,000 people. He is in the eye of every political storm that affects broadcasting. He has to make his command effective throughout the bureaucracy.

It is a job no man could do, and of course no Director-General does it. Impossible jobs tend to be done badly.

The senior managers of the BBC see the Board of Governors as confused, capricious and lacking in professional understanding.

When I was Vice-Chairman I did not, for obvious reasons, often hear the phrase "the nodding Governors", but it seems for a long time to have been a customary description and sums up the managerial frustration. In practice the Governors quite often show better judgement that the professionals.

Nor have the relationships between senior management and the Director General been easy — in the last three years two of the three Managing Directors have been fired, in each case without prior warning.

"By the way, have you ever considered early retirement?" is the Broadcasting House equivalent of the bullet in the back of the head in the Lubianka.

The large BBC bureaucracy lacks anything one could call an enterprise culture. Indeed it has a bias against commercialism, except in terms of the quasi-commercial pursuit of television ratings.

It took five years of campaigning to secure this summer's appointment of a Marketing Director with outside experience. The licence fee provides almost all the BBC's funds and inevitably the power in the BBC bureaucracy belongs not to those who get the revenue, but to those who spend it. And indeed they have used that power to build high standards of production in many areas.

The BBC came into existence because there was a natural monopoly of radio airwaves. There is no longer any natural broadcasting monopoly, though the technologies which have destroyed the monopoly, satellite and cable, are being introduced only gradually.

There is no guarantee that in a fully competitive broadcasting market a state system based on a licence fee will be seen as necessary or even as desirable. Certainly a state monopoly newspaper at a compulsory charge would be regarded as an outrage in every free country.

As broadcasting moves out of the century of monopoly into a new century of competition, the question is whether there will be a place for the BBC and whether the BBC will have the adaptability and energy to fill it. That will depend on what success Mr Hussey has as the architect of necessary change; whether he can make the BBC more open, more adaptable, more enterprising, more effective.

After working with him closely for 12 years I have faith in him, but I know he will have to overcome the resistance of the most heavily bureaucratised system I have ever worked in. As Lord Hill, an earlier Chairman, once said: "The BBC is like the Sargasso Sea; as you move ahead it closes in behind you."

Cracking a great egg-head con trick

Egg-head Mensa-member Peter Marshall says he has encountered discrimination against people with a high IQ. He complains of it. He's about to do three years of research into it. "I have spoken to many university staff," he says, "who have admitted that they treat people with high IQs with caution and suspicion."

My dear old turkey, caution and suspicion scarcely come into it: in my experience, these Denizens are treated with irritation and impatience up to and including physical violence! Imagine having to sit next to one of those bomb-quiz intellectuals at dinner, listening to them windbag away on advertising, and quantum physics, and Manchester United, and whatever else the modish intellectual talks about these days — imagine three courses next to Julian Barnes, or Martin Amis, or the so-called Carmen Callil, you'd pull their noses would you not? You'd take them by the beard and pull their noses!

The gaudy intellectual will invariably come to grief: look at Sir Clive Sinclair — a man so clever his brain actually sticks out of his head, and where, pray, is he now? By contrast, a girl with so fragile an intelligence that she loses a couple of IQ points every time she sneezes — and she, God willing, will be the next Queen of England.

But then the Royal Family has an intuitive grasp of this so-English effect, and they take great pains to conceal their subtle and penetrating minds lest they undermine the great popular appeal of the monarchy. One Sarah Ferguson, you may care to note, latterly suffered from a weakness for Kierkegaard. Her soaring intellect was, however, allied to robust commonsense: a stringent discipline stemmed the flow of mid-nineteenth century Danish quotations demonstrating sin to be alienation from Self, and the rest is history.

You may also be interested to know that Prince Andrew contributes to the New York Review Of Books under a variety of middle European pseudonyms; Prince Edward ("I've got this silly sense of humour") has written several monographs on the psychological imperatives behind the racist joke; and Prince Philip wrote the influential Seven Types Of Ambiguity under the pseudonym William Empson.

But they have seen, Mr so-called Marshall, as any of us do who are genuinely popular and successful, how important it is to stand well at the Long Bar of popular opinion ("Mine's a pint, don't mind if I do"). No one likes a smart-alec, no one trusts a clever-dick. Good manners go further in the world than showing off your intellectual muscles on the academic riviera, my friend. Point taken? Enough said? Excellent then, there it is. And as my friend, the correctively intelligent Barry Norman says, "Another day, another dollar."

Simon Carr

Warning bells

THE Labour Party seems to have allowed itself a fairly leisurely timetable for closing down the British nuclear industry. John Edmonds of the union GMBATU has cheerfully announced, with a twirl of his droopy moustache, that nothing much will happen until "the century after next". But for a moment last week it looked as if we might not have to wait that long. While more than 250 top nuclear engineers and scientists were gathered at a special meeting of the British Nuclear Energy Society for a "technical appraisal" of the accident at Chernobyl, the building's alarms went off.

One hopes that the engineers will react rather more briskly to a nuclear alarm than they did to the frantic calls to evacuate the building. At least one senior official of the National Radiological Protection Board chose that moment to go to the lavatory.

To judge by the number of senior naval personnel present, any fire would have solved Labour's problems over Polaris, too. It turned out, however, that the alarm had been triggered by a short-circuit in the air-conditioning plant.

DIARY

April showers

TALKING of nuclear power, I can reveal (as we diarists like to say) that it didn't rain in the Chernobyl area for more than a month after the accident.

So what? Well, although the area round Chernobyl is heavily contaminated, the pollution is nothing to what it might have been had the rains brought more radioactivity down from the clouds or washed material out of the reactor's core. The Soviet nuclear engineers persuaded their colleagues in the State Committee on Meteorology to "seed" approaching thunderclouds with chemicals that made it rain everywhere other than the Ukrainian plain.

Hard times

ONE of the lonely and unpopular causes I champion is that of Princess Michael. But she certainly doesn't make my task any easier. Interviewed for the November issue of *Good Housekeeping*, the author of *Crowned in a Far Country* tells us about her apartment in Kensington Palace: "My two children are on the top floor but it's such a long way down for little ones to come — yes, like a high-rise flat, exactly". In every particular?

Still, she recovers her form elsewhere in the interview, putting her large feet firmly on the exquisite toes of royal courtier Hugh Casson as she tells of her invitation to talk at the Royal Academy dinner a few years ago. "All the speeches were written by Sir Hugh Casson. Did you know they did that? With brackets for (applause) in them? I said I'm not going unless I can say what I want. And guess who didn't go?"

Blowing bubbles

WHO could fail to be stirred by the speech at Blackpool last week from Robin Cook, Labour's campaign co-ordinator, in which he tellingly noted that champagne imports had trebled in the past couple of years?

But I'm afraid that those responsible for the import boom are not merely cigar-chewing fat-cats or tiara-ed dowagers. Designer socialists, too, are doing their bit. (Even Eric Heffer, who is nobody's idea of a designer socialist, has been known to raise a glass or two of fizz to his lips.) And what were Neil Kinnock and his entourage downing on the train from Blackpool to London last Friday? Bubbly, and in heroic quantities too.

Criminal class

THE law'n'order debate at the Conservative conference, always a rollicking occasion, takes place tomorrow afternoon. But one man who hoped to speak in it may be unavoidably absent. Mark Kotecha, the delegate from Holborn and St Pancras Conservative Association, set off for Bournemouth yesterday morning. He had got no further than the tube station when he gained a valuable insight into inner-city crime: his wallet was nicked. With no money for his train fare, the hapless Kotecha was last seen, still in London, hitch-hiking beside the south circular.

Francis Wheen

LETTERS

Another problem for Reykjavik

Dear sir,

The Iran-Iraq war has now been fuelled over six years. This conflict between two member-states of the United Nations surely represents the most serious breakdown of international order since 1945. Beside it the terrorist operations which so often occupy our headlines are mere peppricks — and even they may in some cases, be partly side-effects of it. I hope also that your newspaper, which sets out with the laudable aim of giving serious coverage of international affairs, will find a way of pressing the apparent indifference of the rest of the world to this horrifying slaughter and concentrating the minds of policy-makers on the search for ways to bring it to an end. I hope also that the leaders of the superpowers meeting in Reykjavik this week, will give this problem more than a token place on their agenda. Critics of the United Nations often — and rightly — cite its inability to halt the Iran-Iraq war as an example of its impotence and inadequacy. But the reason that the powers of enforcement given to the UN in 1945 have never been used (with the single and doubtful exception of Korea) is that they were predicated on the assumption that the great powers would act in concert as they had done against Hitler.

There is no disagreement between the superpowers that I am aware of, either about the rights or wrongs of the Iran-Iraq war or about the terms on which it should be halted. Their inability to take joint action on this, or even stemmed, from sheer distrust of each other. If, as we must all hope, they are now about to establish a better working relationship that should surely cover not only arms control but also the maintenance of world order.

Yours,

EDWARD MORTIMER
Burford, Oxfordshire
October 6

Benefits of boxing

Dear sir,

Like Lloyd Honeyghan, your newspaper has entered the ring with the odds stacked against it. May I first of all congratulate you on your enterprise and hope that you will prove, as he did, that your ability and workrate can be ranked with the best.

Having already revealed my interest in boxing, might I request that The Independent, when judging the pros and cons of this great sport, bears in mind that boxing is a sport inherently an aggressive animal and is not likely to change because of pressures talk. Encouraging the young to be aware of this and get it out of their systems under controlled conditions can only benefit society. Doctors inform us, as if we did not already know, that boxing may damage our health. But with the continual improvement of medical control in the sport, the odd punch-drunk syndrome is all but a necessity. The anti-social aggression of youth is automatically blunted by the numerous dedicated instructors in the amateur clubs throughout Britain. Boys are made aware of the necessity for self-control, discipline and respect for others without which no boxer can succeed. One might hope that other sports would use these principles when training young lads in their recreations.

Perhaps a newspaper such as The Independent might enquire into the reasons for the decrease in sportsmanlike behaviour over the last decade. I look forward to reading articles which give both sides of every argument so that the public can form its own opinion.

Yours faithfully,
BILL SHEERAN
County Wexford, Eire
September 30

Feathered fiends

Dear sir,

I note with some foreboding that you have chosen the eagle to decorate your masthead. Are you aware of the habits of this pestilential bird? It is, to be brief, the image of male chauvinism: a predator that does not incubate or feed its young (although it does collect their food), it feeds on others of its species, not to mention sickly young lambs which it seizes by the head and haunches. Of course, it is territorially aggressive — when it is not indulging its habitual lethargy — and, like man, it only moves gracefully when it takes to the air.

Yours faithfully,
AMANDA MATTHEWS
Birkenhead, Cheshire
October 4

Press siege in Chile

Dear sir,

The intolerable nature of the current human rights situation in Chile was recently brought to our attention once more when the military junta imposed a state of siege on September 8. Since that date, at least four people, one of them a prominent journalist, whose only crime was to tell the truth, have been dragged from their homes and murdered. Six opposition magazines have been shut down, and many leaders of the opposition have been arrested. There are strong fears for their safety, since they are in the hands of the Chilean police, who have a record of brutality, and who have been invested with special powers under the state of siege.

Here in Britain the press is fortunate enough to enjoy a freedom of expression denied to the Chilean media. I wish you well with your new venture and look forward to seeing this freedom utilised to the utmost.

Yours faithfully,
MANUEL SEPULVEDA
Co-ordinator
Chile Democration
London, EC1
October 2

Listening in

Dear sir,

The recent High Court ruling in the CND telephone-tapping case gives the impression that private communications in Britain are only intercepted on the authority of warrants issued in the names of specific individuals. This is untrue.

The Home Office often issues warrants in the name of an organisation thus enabling Special Branch and MI5 to tap the telephones of any number of people who may be associated, however loosely, with this grouping. Incidentally, tapping call boxes does not require a warrant, nor does the acquisition of telephone numbers called by a subscriber from their local exchange.

Additionally, the Foreign Office intercepts every telephone and telex call, privately leased circuit, cable, and data transmission, entering and leaving Britain or using the domestic microwave trunk network. This illegal practice began in July 1919 when the then Home Secretary signed a directive claiming that an emergency had arisen, thus enabling him to use his catch-all powers of interception under the amended Official Secrets Act of 1912.

The scope of this operation, which has now become a joint Anglo-American affair, is so vast that computers are used to search for specific names, numbers, addresses, and even "trigger words" in the messages that are of interest to MI5, MI6, and the CIA.

Yours faithfully,
JAMES RUSBRIDGER
St Austell, Cornwall
September 30

Perils of Labour's re-nationalisation

Dear sir,

I have been watching with interest the efforts of the Labour Party to come to terms with the fact that over 12 per cent of the voters in Britain are enjoying the benefits of various stores towards wider share ownership. It must be the mark of a growing sense of tradition that the Party leaders have tried to change the outdated image of the old Clause IV nationalisation argument into a more palatable formula. If the change of heart is to be seen as more than an election ploy, however, there still has to be some serious re-thinking about the ideas of rationalising the British Telecom and British Gas shareholdings in a 'bonds for shares' swap.

The millions of ordinary citizens who bought shares in British Telecom and who are about to do so in British Gas have made their views known about the failure of the old style nationalised industry, which is fickle and indecisive operated by the needs of the new venture. The Labour Party will need more than dogma to prove its case against British Telecom and British Gas shareholders, who are, and who insists, that their involvement should be better not be re-nationalised.

At stake is something which is damaging about the spread of wider share ownership as a means of making conspicuous the British Telecom and British Gas can now re-possess to the needs of the community, which of rebalancing shares

holders, who are consumers and employees, about the commercial requirements of such a company. Wider share ownership brings greater understanding of the prime importance of industry and commerce to our quality of life. This quality is determined by the efficiency of management, by incentives, by goods and services produced, by marketing, by after sales service, and by industrial relations.

If, as I suspect, the Labour Party's plans for British Telecom and British Gas cannot provide the same degree of participation and involvement through nationalisation as wider share ownership has brought, then it is time that they addressed the fact. If the Party can shed this last vestige of the old hard-line approach, then it may be possible to turn Clause IV with the total Branch directive, giving it a firely workman down, despite the damage it has done to our economy.

Yours faithfully
SIR NICHOLAS GOODISON
Chairman of The Stock Exchange
London, EC2
October 6

The Independent welcomes letters from readers. Letters for publication should be addressed to the Letters Editor, and should include the writer's address, together with a daytime telephone number.

The face of Tory rule after Thatcher?

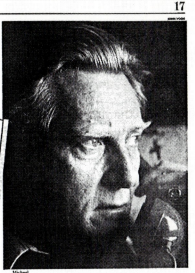

Michael Heseltine:
Dramatic prescription for a brave new Britain

Michael Heseltine is not a man given to hesitation, but there was a distinct and loaded pause when he was asked whether he had been approached to challenge Margaret Thatcher for the leadership. The silence was also heavy when he was asked to explain what the Conservative Party owed the Prime Minister.

The former Secretary of State for Defence, who resigned over the Westland affair, is now creating his own personal manifesto for the leadership contest which he believes will take place when Mrs Thatcher stands down sometime after the next election, leaving obtained an overall majority of between 30 and 40 seats in the new Parliament.

He is preparing a book for publication next year and at this week's party conference he is expected to use a fringe meeting on Thursday as his platform for controversial views on the future of the Conservative Party and the country.

So had he been asked to stand for the leadership in advance of the election? "People make all sorts of suggestions, but my own view is that the Prime Minister will lead the Conservatives into the next election and that she will win."

Mrs Thatcher would win by between 30 and 40 seats because of three factors. "One, that the broad economic background against which the election will be fought is one of rising living standards for a very significant proportion of the population, based upon very low levels of inflation and very high pay settlements. Secondly, the incredibility of Labour's defence policy and, thirdly, that the British people are broadly democratically stable and there is no precedent for overwhelming a majority of the size that this Government has got in one election."

A third Tory term of government provides the foundation for Mr Heseltine's dramatic prescription for Whitehall and the country: a manifesto which would give greater importance to the Department of Trade and Industry than to the Treasury, and to a switch of public subsidy away from mortgages and pensions into industrial and wealth-creating investment.

At the very top of his list of priorities is an industrial strategy. "It would start with a shake-up, a re-alignment of the forces of power within government, a significant diminution of the role of the Treasury, which I think is an historic anachronism within this country.

"Other countries, the capitalist

Michael Heseltine talks exclusively to Anthony Bevins about the future of the Conservative Party

economies with which we must compete, have all harnessed their resources, into a far more cohesive partnership to address the national interest and to attack the world's markets. That is the issue we have to address.

"The Secretary of State for Trade and Industry should be one of the most important people in the Government, should chair a Cabinet committee responsible for the excellence of our wealth-creating abilities and should draw together the dialogue between shareholders, managers and workers in a way that the present structure of Whitehall frustrates.

"The Treasury talks to the Bank of England and the Bank of England talks to the institutions and the shareholders, and the Department of Trade and Industry in a different world. It's unthinkable that you can pursue an industrial policy of excellence if the shareholders are not deeply committed to its success."

So where would the capital come from for this grand design? "We have to examine the incentives that exist within society in Britain and which have the effect of undermining the strength of the provincial industrial base and drawing the savings of the British people through the institutions of the City, often into areas of investment which are not concerned with wealth-creation."

Such as? "Mortgage tax relief is a major subsidy of £4.75bn to the house-building industry which has immense consequences for the insurance companies which provide the cover for the mortgages, and the flow of savings through to the insurance companies is southern-orientated and leads to an investment profile that is very far from being directed to wealth-creating purposes.

"About £3.5bn worth of subsidy goes to encourage companies to invest through pension funds which enjoy tax-free income, but which again are centralised, and invest with statutorily-imposed caution very significantly in areas which are not pre-eminently concerned with wealth creation.

"If you are looking for a shift of the nation's endeavours into wealth-creating activities, you have to look at the scale of those subsidies. I am not suggesting that overnight they all disappear, but if governments are prepared to intervene on that scale as they do, there's no earthly reason why the intervention shouldn't be directed into more wealth-creating activities."

For a Conservative to talk of transferring more than £8bn in subsidies away from his party's own power-bases into industry and the deprived areas of the North, as Mr Heseltine does, is brave indeed. What, then does he envisage for pension reliefs?

"You could give the same incentives to the companies as you give to the pension funds, or you could take the pension fund incentives away."

Mortgage relief? "You could introduce tax-exempt bonds for investment in inner-city regeneration."

But behind the Heseltine manifesto for reform there lies a concern about unemployment. "The social consequences of levels of unemployment which genuinely deny the opportunity to work are unacceptable. They threaten the basic social values, human values, family values, on which the Tory party places great reliance.

"But to confuse the circumstances of big urban industrial areas in the North-east and central cities like Glasgow, Manchester, Liverpool, with conditions that apply in my constituency of Henley is grossly unforgiveable.

"The subalterns are not industrial solutions, they are local solutions. In the stress areas you have to be generous, concerned, understanding, and you have to pursue policies which will cost money, public money. No party is offering a solution that significantly reduces the levels of unemployment in the stress areas.

"You don't address the problem by saying we'll get rid of a million unemployed. You're still going to leave the ghetto society with all the social deprivation and the crime consequences that follow.

"But if you're not prepared to accept the hope that something will get better, and you want policies to ensure they get better, then you have to combine a more vigorous discipline in the

non stress areas of the prosperous parts of the country with a more generous policy in the areas where the stress is of a totally different nature.

"In real terms today those who are managing the unemployed are simply managing a process of handing out cheques. Equally, the financial incentives to work are so narrow for so many people that it is unrealistic to think that a significant number of people are going to do it. And you're therefore left with not only a need for a tighter administration, but with the need to question whether people shouldn't be expected to give something in return for the unemployment benefits that they receive. I think that what we have got to find is a range — at one end of the scale training schemes, at the other end of the scale, actually useful activities which in the non-stress parts of the country are part of the process of an employment entitlement."

Such schemes would apply to his own Oxfordshire constituency of Henley, where 1.9% were claiming benefit in August — the twelfth best-off constituency in Britain as far as unemployment was concerned.

Housing investment and education are two other areas of concern for Mr Heseltine. Although he dismisses labels, he would, like many of his colleagues on the left of the Conservative Party, invest in the housing stock.

"At his ideas about education, while pulling short of the right-wing Mrs Thatcher group, do smack of similar radical reform. "The central thrust is to put an enhanced weight upon the heads of schools. That will involve paying more, but using much more widely the concept of contract in terms of employment, and to delegate far more power to schools.

"There is one other thing which, in the normal sowthingness of Britain to come to terms with public expenditure extravagance, we will not be able to grasp. And that is the recent Audit Commission report showing something of the order of £300m worth of economies to be achieved if schools were brought down in number to fit the number of pupils for whom there is an educational need. If we try to bulldoze the closure programme through, we will meet every sort of local resistance, if we try to do it slowly, the worst in the process will be spiralling and I would myself be looking for an alternative which met with the grain of both parents and teachers' ambitions.

"If there is £300m or anything like it available, and I think there is, we ought to look for a way of putting most of that money on the table for improved conditions and standards of education providing that the rationalisation in debt or what money's on the table is linked to expenditures I don't think it is beyond the wit of government to do that."

Lessons the party must learn

Walk out: Michael Heseltine quits the cabinet over the Westland row

ALTHOUGH Mr Heseltine's clash with Mrs Thatcher over the Westland affair led to his resignation, surely he and the party owe a debt to the woman who — as he firmly believes — will win a third term in office?

The question prompted an uncharacteristic pause. "She has led the party at a time when significant change and achievements lie to the credit of the Conservative Party. Historically, bringing the unions within the law of the land, I think, will be a permanent and historic landmark.

"I don't think that will ever be reversed. That is a huge achievement, which curiously enough Barbara Castle and Harold Wilson embarked on with their White Paper In Place of Strife in the Sixties, Ted Heath addressed in the early Seventies and, under this Government, has been finally resolved.

"The most interesting evolution under this Government has been the process of privatisation. As we have gone on and as the public have come to realise the benefits of privatisation — particularly with council housing — so the Government's confidence and ambitions have grown."

But Mr Heseltine believes past successes do not entitle the party to become complacent, and changes must be made in the light of crumbling support in urban areas.

"The party cannot countenance a situation where we control no large city, where we have to fight our way back to the provincial high-ground of this country. We have to have something to say at

to why these parts of Britain which were once Tory-controlled should reconsider the Conservative option. Because we can't retreat into the strongholds of the south of England."

Mr Heseltine believes that the aims he has outlined could be achieved only by a Conservative government, but he will not be drawn on whether he is the only leader who could drive it through.

But did he believe that the Conservative Party would eventually turn its back on the present political style of Mrs Thatcher? He is tactful. "Well, I don't

think that's on the agenda at the moment."

After the election? He laughs: "You won't get me to speculate about that issue. My concern is to do everything I can to get the party to win the election. Tomorrow is another day."

But if and when Mrs Thatcher went, would he be a candidate? "Oh Lord, I would be as interested in the leadership of the Conservative Party as virtually every other member of the Cabinet."

The race for the succession may well begin this week in Bournemouth.

Prior's great adventure that never began

BOOK REVIEW

A BALANCE OF POWER
Jim Prior
Hamish Hamilton
£12.95
388pp

JIM PRIOR was always the plausible politician and now in A Balance of Power he has written the plain man's account of the plain man's life. The title of his book usefully reminds any reader who has forgotten that politics, particularly at Cabinet level, is a business of checks and balances. Prior's account of his career has many virtues, but Mr Prior's account of his own political career is a refreshingly direct one. Reading Mr Prior's long-looks it is difficult to remember that a great adventure ever began.

His Prior always strikes me as real political danger in the Tory party is a dull, well-meaning man of the provincial middle-ground. Jim Prior's account of his career is a refreshingly direct one. Reading Mr Prior's long-looks it is difficult to remember that a great adventure ever began.

His Prior always strikes me as the straightest and the pragmatist: a appears at its best form. A Balance of Power reveals something only a man of his calibre and of the original contest Margaret Thatcher's programme knew and only complacent optimism was marked by the regular renewal

prize pig at the local agricultural show. Indeed, Mr Prior shows more life in describing how he fought to qualify as an official pig keeper during his days at Charterhouse school than he does in chronicling the his-tory conduct which the Conservative Party in which he took part. With the pigs he was. With the Conservatives he lost.

Reading his account of the Tory conflicts it is difficult to understand why communion and contempts like Margaret Thatcher stood beneath this chariot wheels opponents who believed that the destiny of the Tories is to do what is best in the circumstances and accept that we live in an imperfect world.

I speak of the battles between the romantics and the pragmatists. It appears at its best form. A Balance of Power had adventures only flowed on only side of the original contest Margaret Thatcher's programme knew and only complacent optimism was marked by the regular renewal

of "wets" cither from his Cabinet or in economically insignificant posts within it. As part of that process, Mr Prior was shuffled from the Department of Employment to the Northern Ireland Office. His account of the years in that so much bland as complacent: "The way I played the reshuffle and subsequent events consider ably weakened my authority, and also the cause of wider states-in-the-conservative backbenches I was not mesmerised by the Prime Minister as is probably why she was Prime Minister and I was certainly never likely to be.

Charitable readers than who do not interpret that episode to Mr Prior's happier we all conclude that he is a pragmatist a reluctant that who prefers to go with the tide rather than resist it. But it offers a flow as it struck with getting power but Prior's factories I and Corruption are described as only best foreign Secretary they seemed to be write

about other colleagues in a way which he must know they will find painfully offensive. Sir Keith Joseph's description matches super-literal affection and deep criticism in equal measure.

This thoroughly honourable man was not suited to the age of partisan Minister. He made heavy weather of everything he touched from the Health Service in the early 70s, through industry to Higher Education in the 80s. He moved awkwardly and indecisive while taking on the concern moving from one brief to another. He often got so others did simply for want of an alternative period of power his pulling at party-back from instrument and mislaid side. Too often they are charmed and simply from want of an alternative posed attempt at real rationalisation. Mr Prior's successor was asked through expeditures I don't think it is beyond the wit of government to do that.

Roy Hattersley

Prior: "was commissioned by the Prime Minister"

reader the ability to study the details at leisure and in depth.

The reproduction of the colour photograph varied from plant to plant – a fact we had become used to with some advertisements. The readers seemed to like the colour photograph; there were many requests to buy a colour print of it in the following days. We were to remain cautious about the use of editorial colour thereafter, only using it a handful of times in the first year.

By that date as well, the Lifestyle page of earlier times had become Living and appeared as a page in its own right on Mondays and Fridays. Fashion appeared under its aegis and was not to have a separate identity for some time. This practice was often questioned and the answer lay in the much earlier decision to try to keep issues relating to life, or lifestyle or style under one banner. It was a conscious effort to provide something new without the customary labels which could discourage male readers. It was a brave attempt which did not catch on and illustrated once again the innate conservatism of many readers at the quality end of the market. Later when Suzy Menkes joined the newspaper (26 May 1987) from *The Times*, the well-established Fashion Page was back and the advertising started to flow in.

I had been very anxious in the months before launch that the Weekend pages should have and retain a different perspective on layout. In June 1986, preliminary plans had been laid to have a separate Weekend section appearing on a Saturday. From my experience at *The Times*, where I edited the Saturday section for two years, I knew that if the right editorial and design was there, advertisers would become attracted to it and, as the bandwagon rolled, more editorial space would be generated. Initially, I had to resist my inclinations to carry different typefaces in the section. It might have worked if it had been a pull-out section but not as an integral part of the main paper.

Despite using the same typeface, the way to distinguish the section seemed to be to label or signpost it in a distinctive way; Hilly Janes, the editor of the section, and I agreed that Michael Daley, an artist I had managed to lure away from the *Sunday Times* and the *Financial Times*, should draw the logos. He has a fine detailed style, building up his drawings almost through a pointillist technique. His hand-drawn logos have given the section great appeal and emphasised once again the importance of separating and announcing different elements of a newspaper.

The layout has remained adventurous in the use of photographs, maps and boxes for displaying factual material.

As the first year progressed, *The Independent* advanced on all fronts – in editorial terms it displayed a healthy desire to expose fraud (The Guinness scandal), to publish open secrets (Peter Wright and *Spycatcher*, his book about the British Secret Service), to identify humbug (by remaining out of the Lobby system), to reveal the truth behind Government assurances (the state of the National Health Service) and to stand up for journalistic freedom. The united commitment of its journalists reaffirmed the view that there was no substitute for experience at the highest level. But behind the high profile gloss, mistakes were made, stories missed and deadlines broken – just like any other newspaper. Some staff have left – notably Douglas Long who retired as managing director at the end of 1986, shortly before his 62nd birthday. AWS assumed the role of chief executive as well as editor.

On the advertising front, display matched and then broke target figures. Classified remained a problem throughout the year but gradually picked up sales and by November 1987 was not far short of its targets. Working closely with a design company called Tango, a subsidiary of *The Independent's* new advertising agency, Barton, Bogle, Hegarty, I helped to redesign the advertising page layout in late autumn 1987. It was a part of the design equation that traditionally was left to outsiders and to the advertising department to control. For years there had been a distinct separation between advertising and editorial affairs. To some advertising staff, editorial was provided to fill up the space between the advertisements, to some journalists advertising was a necessary evil that paid their salaries and enabled them to enjoy a decent standard of living. On *The Independent* there was far more contact between the two groups. As a result 90 per cent of the design work for advertising, marketing and promotion is carried out through the design department. Without any conscious articulation, a corporate image for the newspaper has been established in visual, design terms through in-house commitment.

The new design had to reflect the strong growth of classified advertising over the year and once again provide better sign-posting for the multifarious advertising headings. My original designs with a sans serif heading carried with a centred rule each side was a conscious effort to distinguish the newspaper from *The Times* which carried an elegant shadow box around its advertisement headings. On the text side, Clarendon provided the right answer (see chapter 7) and was to remain the standard typeface for the 'smalls'.

In the end we settled on a far more reserved look for advertising headings using a main headline in Century to announce the subject of the page, for example, Appointments followed by the sub-section headings in a smaller Century headline ruled off on a grey tint background. Further down the scale in classified terms, the subject headings are in a box with a thicker rule below, which draws the reader's eye down to the actual words of the advertisement. The classified columns are now separated by 1pt vertical rules. So much for the typography. On the layout side of advertising pages I have now encouraged the use of horizontal techniques which adhere to the principles of modularity as much as possible. The overall effect of this unannounced change is to give the advertising pages a cleaner, more reserved appearance. This in turn improves the prospects for more advertising. The medium is the message for the media. This change was another consolidation of the design process.

Overleaf, the leader spread on 5 January 1988.

THE INDEPENDENT
40 CITY ROAD LONDON EC1Y 2DB Telephone 01 253 1222. Telex 9419611 INDPNT

America's uncertain disapproval

TIME, tough Israeli control, and harsh economic necessity have combined to bring to a temporary end the wave of unrest in the Gaza Strip and the West Bank. Yet it is certain that the protests will erupt again if nothing is done to remove the root cause of the trouble: the 20 year-old occupation by Israel of Palestinian territory. Given that certainty, the minimum that Israel should do is what it has so signally failed to do up to now: form, train and equip a force capable of dealing with riots without resorting to firearms.

Faced with trouble from orthodox Jews in Jerusalem, the police there were able to contain them without firing a shot. But in Gaza and the other occupied areas, the policing is done by the young recruits of the army or by the Druse Border Police, a force which has earned itself a deserved reputation for ruthlessness. In the case of the army, the young soldiers are sent into a hostile environment with no protective shields or clothing, and often in small patrols. The result is that when confronted by stone-throwing mobs, they resort too soon to their guns. The activities of the discredited internal security force, Shin Bet, have also done little to help matters.

In Washington, the White House went much further than usual in criticising Israel for its tactics, saying: "Demonstrations and riots on one side and harsh security measures and the excessive use of live ammunition on the other cannot substitute for genuine dialogue." By the normal standard of American-Israeli relations, these were hard words and it quickly drew from American-Jewish leaders a knee-jerk denunciation of PLO terrorists and fundamentalists. There was no further comment from the White House. In an election year, the Jewish lobby is even more influential than usual, and the fact that President Reagan is not standing makes little difference: he and his advisers must still do all they can to ensure the succession of a fellow Republican — an end which would not be assisted by offending those many American Jews who have only recently deserted the Democratic Party.

It would, however, almost certainly be possible for the Reagan administration to put greater pressure on Israel without alienating American-Jewish voters. They, like everyone else, have been horrified by the television images of Israeli troops clubbing or shooting women and children — pictures, incidentally, often taken by Israeli cameramen and allowed out by the Israeli censors in a way which virtually no other Middle Eastern country would countenance. If President Reagan were to insist that some of the vast American aid to Israel, both military and civil, were to be allocated for riot shields, water cannon and tear gas, he might save some Palestinian lives, prevent the increasing brutalisation of the Israeli Army, and salve the conscience of some American Jews. If at the same time he were to urge the Israelis to participate in the sort of international conference which seems the only way a lasting peace may yet be gained, then President Reagan would go into the the history books for something even bolder than the prospective agreement with Mr Gorbachev to halve the number of strategic nuclear weapons.

Limits on the right to abortion

THE report on BBC Radio 4's *Today* programme that pregnant women, having discovered their foetusesare female, sometimes choose to have them aborted, will shock many who support the "woman's right to choose". The knowledge that a foetus is male or female is gained by tests usually carried out to discover whether serious abnormalities exist. To discover that a foetus seems perfectly healthy, and then to carry out an abortion solely on grounds of sex, is to misuse information intended only to prevent the birth of grievously handicapped children.

Not only is it repugnant to most people in this country to abort a child for this reason: it is illegal. To reduce the danger that a doctor may unwittingly help a mother to break the law, it should be good professional practice, enforced by the British Medical Association, not to tell the parents of an expected child what its sex is, when that information is irrelevant to the child's general health.

Beyond that point, and the need for greater professional vigilance, the report points to a wider difficulty about the way the debate on abortion is liable to be conducted. Moral absolutists will seize on it as evidence for their argument that once abortions are allowed for any reason but to save the mother's life, a slippery slope has been embarked upon. They will say that just as there is no moral distinction between killing a crippled adult and a healthy one, so there is none between killing crippled and healthy foetuses. They will argue that having become used to aborting the severely handicapped, because looking after them will be a terrible burden, it should be easy enough to become used to aborting girls, because providing dowries for them will be a terrible burden. The idea that any child who does not fulfil his or her parents' desires should not be born will have taken hold, at the expense of the idea that any child is unique and precious and to be loved unconditionally.

Not the least error in stating the case against abortion in such terms is that it impugns the motives of those who support the existing law governing abortion. It implies that they are a callous, selfish, wicked lot. Since many of them are moved by feelings of compassion, and by knowledge of cases of terrible suffering which they wish to prevent recurring, this imputation is as unfair as it is unproductive of intelligent debate.

But the present controversy indicates that some of those who believe that abortion should in particular circumstances be allowed can also be guilty of overstating their case. The woman's right to choose must be qualified by anyone who thinks a woman should not be able to choose an abortion because the child's gender does not suit her. And even if the slogan was not open to that objection, it is flawed because it suggests that those who oppose abortion must be illiberal, determined on the oppression of women. Since some of them think they are safeguarding the liberties of the foetus, that imputation is as unwarranted as the imputation of selfishness to supporters of abortion. It is one thing to say your opponents are wrong, quite another to suggest that they are evil. Few debates on public policy are as disfigured by emotional slander as that over the rights and wrongs of abortion.

MRS T IS
DELIBERATELY
UNREASONABLE
EMOTIONAL
EXCITABLE
10
PERSONALITY
CULT
THIS IS A
CENTRALIST
AUTHORITARIAN
GOVERNMENT
THE CABINET IS
JUST A RUBBER STAMP
Garland

"YOU SEE GRAFFITI ON WALLS. IT IS HORRID, YOU CANNOT BLAME GOVERNMENTS FOR THIS."

What the lay Establishment thinks of the Church's troubles

The Church of England still excites interest, says William Rees-Mogg

What does the lay Establishment think of the Church of England? I spent the last days of the old year and the first day of 1987 trying to find out. I rang a number of my friends, men and women who run or have run businesses, public institutions, media, farms, schools, or libraries. None of them are clergy, or members of the Synod. They veer towards conservatism, though most are well to the left of Mrs Thatcher. They are for the most part middle-aged. They are all Anglicans, though one is an agnostic Anglican. Most of them are regular church-goers.

It was very striking how interested they all were in the subject. The conversations were lively, vivid and tended to be prolonged. They were speaking off the record, in that I was not going to name them individually, but they wanted to express their views. If I had rung the same group to ask their opinions about the future of the Government or the poll tax or the National Health Service, the conversations would have been briefer and less animated. Whatever may be the problems of the Church of England, it has not ceased to be an institution which arouses intense interest.

All of the respondents agreed on one theme, though on almost everything else they disagreed. They distrusted and disliked the Synod, and thought that the Synod had opened up a gap between the general body of church-goers and the Church of England as an institution. "The Church of England has allowed its busier and more sensible elements to be squeezed out by its dottier and less employable elements," was one way of putting it.

The Synod was seen as a 1960s type of false democratisation which had replaced the authority of the bishops with "a body of busybodies". It destroyed the Church's lines of command. Most of the respondents, though not all, thought that the Church of England was "an institution in crisis"; all of them thought that the Synod was an inappropriate form of government which had contributed to such a crisis.

They had criticisms of the bishops, but they would prefer to see the bishops run the Church. The Synod is also blamed by those who deplore the loss of the old liturgy.

The second issue which was repeatedly raised, usually with no prompting from me, was the question of homosexuality. I had rather thought that this was a question exaggerated by the press, but it seems to be at the front of people's minds.

"The idea is getting around that the Church of England is in favour of homosexuality," was immediately followed by a partial retraction. But there seems to be a widespread opinion that the Synod debate was a disaster. The Establishment view, and perhaps more generally the lay Anglican view, is that the clergy must not sleep with other men, or women other than their wives. It is as simple as that.

On the other hand, one respondent, who has two homes, has a gay vicar in London and a heterosexual vicar in the country. The gay vicar, to the best of his knowledge, is gay in orientation but not in practice. He contrasts him, a deeply religious Anglo Catholic who has a large and faithful congregation, with the married clergyman and his half-empty church. Though both in his view are good men, it is the homosexual he regards as the more inspiring man of religion.

The issue of women priests divides the respondents and it is this divisiveness which they most fear. One of them, when in New York, looked up the nearest Episcopalian church in the *Yellow Pages*. He found one on Madison Avenue and received communion from a black woman priest. He had no doubt of the validity of the sacrament and regards women priests as becoming a non-issue. Yet others see this as an issue which is destined to tear the Church of England apart, and believe that the Church of England has no right to decide the matter in separation from the Roman Catholic and Orthodox Churches.

On the whole, the Archbishop of Canterbury is much more strongly and warmly supported than one might suppose from recent press comment. It says something for the reach of his work that several of my respondents know him personally, as I do myself. He is criticised for his voice, described as "reedy", for being too cautious, or too political, or "wet". But these criticisms are more than offset by often quite heated praise.

Characteristically, one experienced teacher sees the Archbishop as "extremely honest, sensitive to the feelings of ordinary people, who does a lot of good things very privately and has an incredibly difficult job. The criticisms are very unfair indeed." Another, who has known the Archbishop well, says: "I'm a fan of Bob Runcie's; he's a man of principle. He is the Rab Butler of the Church; he believes in 'the art of the possible'."

Yet another says that he "admires Runcie", and argues that those who do not "misunderstand the nature of the Anglican Church. The Church of England is not dogmatic. It has no supreme pontiff. It is inconceivable that the Archbishop of Canterbury could speak *ex cathedra*. If he tried, the Church would split into 50 pieces." The Falklands sermon is thought to have offended some Conservatives, but is generally defended as a natural Christian response — indeed based on the Lord's Prayer.

The other bishops, particularly the inner-city group, are not so highly regarded. There is an anxiety that there are too few future leaders among them.

On one wing, Dr Leonard — whom I personally admire — tends to be thought of as a maverick rather than as the leader of traditional Anglicanism which many would now look for. The inner-city bishops are seen as having "swallowed the whole Labour Party package" for urban regeneration.

One independent schoolteacher found himself protesting to one of these bishops: "Even if you're dealing with fee-payers, they still have souls." These bishops, like the Synod, are regarded as over-politicised; one even referred to them as "proletarianised".

The Bishop of Durham comes in for general criticism; indeed, he is an issue in himself. The ordinary church-goer wants bishops to teach faith, not to spread doubt. On the other hand, David Sheppard, the Bishop of Liverpool, is widely respected for his faith, even by those who disapprove of his political views.

Traditionally, the Church of England has been strengthened by the support of a Christian lay establishment, with experience and influence well outside Church matters. That support is still there.

But as one of the respondents said: "Nine-tenths of regular church-goers are conservative in tendency and view the antics of the inflated minorities with amusement and horror. That is not what the Church is about."

MILES KINGTON

Television epic on a low budget

IN CASE you missed it, here is an exclusive transcript of Sunday's block busting TV programme about the BBC called *A block busting TV programme about the BBC*.

A whirling globe, marked BBC, slowly comes to rest. It opens, and out steps a white haired businessman in a sober suit. It is Dr Who. No, hold on, it's Duke Hussey. Duke Who?

Duke: Hello. My name is Duke Who. I am chairman of the BBC and I would like to tell you where your licence fee money goes.

Caption flashes up, reading: "This bit of the film was shot on location in Duke's house. It cost nothing." Cut to a man looking tense, sitting in the Mastermind black chair.

DG: Hello. My name is Michael Checkland and tonight I would like to answer questions on my specialist subject, which is, Being DG of the BBC.

Duke: Your first question is, where does all the money go?

A caption flashes up reading: "During the 1987 election night programme David Dimbleby ate more than 7,000 Mars bars."

DG: That's a good question. Let's have a look at this diagram.

An enormous computer graphic diagram flashes up, saying TV 30 per cent, Radio 10 per cent, Wogan's salary 20 per cent, and computer graphics 20 per cent.

DG: Now, we could have got an independent producer to take an independent look at the BBC and ask some searching questions, but that would have cost money. Your money. Instead, Duke Who and I have agreed to appear tonight absolutely free.

Duke: Later, you can phone in and criticise my tie.

A caption flashes up: "Duke's Tie won more than 30 international awards last year". Cut to Mel Smith and Griff Rhys Jones.

Mel: What do you think of this new team, then?

Griff: Great! What new team?

Mel: Duke and Mike.

Griff: What do they do, then?

Mel: Well, they sort of look really intense in close-up and talk obsessively about TV programmes and nod in agreement the whole time.

Griff: Just like us. Sounds great.

Mel: You won't say that when you see them.

Cut to a rocky location somewhere on the Mediterranean. A TV producer is shouting to make himself heard above the wind.

Producer: We're here to make an episode of *Duke and Mike*. Unfortunately, the wind is so bad today that the film crew keeps falling over. A lost day like this could cost us £12,000. Of course, that's true of every film company, not just the BBC, but that's what I've been told to say. OK, tea break, everyone.

Caption flashes up saying: "Flashing up a caption like this takes three men working five days and costs £250,000. Most of that goes on tea breaks". Cut to Michael Fish.

Fish: ... and severe gales. There won't be severe gales, actually, but ever since we got that hurricane so badly wrong, we've been forecasting severe gales every day just to be on the safe side. It costs no more than forecasting good weather, after all. And now it's about time we said something about radio.

Caption flashes past: "The BBC has 440 local radio stations with almost as many listeners." Cut to Duke Who.

Duke: Well, that's enough about radio, I think. Later we'll have shots of Derek Jameson looking intense, Brian Redhead looking tired and some DJ with lots of records rubbing his eyes. We call this 'going behind the scenes', and I often wonder if it fools anyone. Now, here's Sue Lawley to prove that we have women working for us as well.

Sue: Hello. Working on BBC news is tremendously exciting. What happens is this. First, the news happens. Then we find out about it. Then we tell you about it, after which we all rub our eyes and look very tired but happy, unless we've just forecast Mrs Thatcher's election result so badly wrong that even Peter Snow looks surprised.

Duke: In 1987 lots of other things happened. Norman Tebbit gave us a roasting at election time.

DG: We lost Michael Grade just as we were going to make him the big boy.

Duke: We had a most amazing punch-up at Christmas time between the news chief and BBC 1's controller.

DG: And if this were being made by an independent producer, we'd hear all about it.

Duke: But it isn't and we won't.

DG: So now it's time for you to phone in and ask us any questions about anything you like, except all those things we can't talk about.

Caller: I just want to say that where I live, I can't get BBC 1, so I didn't see the programme.

DG: I think that shows we're getting the mix about right.

Caption flashes up: "Please tell all your friends how cheap this programme was to make."

The death of design

BOOK REVIEW

THE GREAT ENGINEERS
Ed: Derek Walker
Academy £35

THOUGH none of the million and a half Londoners who thronged the streets to watch his state funeral was to realise it, the death of the Duke of Wellington marked also the death of the industrial spirit in Britain.

His hearse exemplified, in bronze and gilt, some of the forces that were to bring about the decline. The contract to design and build a funeral car fit to bear the Iron Duke's remains went to the School of Design.

The School had been founded in 1837 with the intention that "the direct application of the arts to manufactures should be deemed an essential element" but in its first 14 years of existence it had had little impact on manufacturing industry.

In 1852, the School had a new and energetic General Superintendent of Practical Art, and the contract for the Duke's funeral car was his chance to prove that art, design and manufacturing could all be harmoniously wedded. Within the allotted three weeks, the extraordinary vehicle was ready: 27 feet long, 10 feet wide and 17 feet high. It got stuck in a gutter by the side of the Mall. The vehicle was too heavy; the wheels and the wheelbase too narrow. As a piece of engineering, it was a failure.

It took the army, police, bystanders and 12 horses more than 15 minutes to pull the hearse clear of the mud. Thereafter, the *Illustrated London News* noted that "it was drawn along with sufficient rapidity to prevent a scrutiny of its design". One bystander, however, had the chance to study the stranded vehicle and was less than impressed by the "horrible South Kensington catalogue with all its tawdry vulgarities".

As a work of art, it seems, the funeral car was a failure too.

The gulf between the arts and industry in Britain curiously mirrors that between science and industry that allegedly concerns our present political leaders. The failure to marry art and industry, to develop an English tradition of design engineering, is visible around us today in, for example, barely habitable buildings that were new only two decades ago, or in motor cars that are the product of an industry that has persistently failed to innovate.

According to *The Great Engineers*, the emphasis of British design has been "on ephemera and front-front." Slick presentation masks impoverished content: the design of useful objects is neglected and instead, British design concentrates on fashion and marketing.

Having metamorphosed into the Royal College of Art, the School of Design is celebrating its 150th anniversary with an exhibition of "The Art of British Engineers". In parallel with the exhibition, Derek Walker, who is Professor of Architecture and Design at the College, has persuaded eminent engineers, designers and industrialists to contribute to this lavishly illustrated book.

But the title is misleading. The book concentrates on structural and civil engineering. Where, one asks, are the mechanical engineers? The biographical appendix includes an entry for Sir John Cockroft, a nuclear physicist, but has none for Lord Hinton of Bankside, this country's finest nuclear engineer. Sir Alec Issigonis, designer of the Morris Minor and the Mini, gets no mention.

The book tells how the past 150 years have seen the triumph of those who believe that "creativity" is the exclusive preserve of people with an arts training. To the British, "progress" is suspect and technology is something that must be tamed and controlled, largely by imposing standards of visual appearance that comply with criteria set up by those who have studied the arts. These tendencies have intensified, not diminished, as Ted Happold, professor of engineering and architecture at Bath university, remarks:

"I sometimes wonder if we were not almost fatally damaged by the refugees from Hitler's Europe. Those who were gifted designers, frustrated by the reactionary environment here, went on to the USA and revolutionised design there. The art critics and historians, discovering our conservative, class-rich environment, stayed on to become famous and powerful in our establishment."

Happold and Walker want to liberate Britain from the "Historic ideas of art and culture [that] can entrap. It is technology that frees the scene."

Tom Wilkie

LETTERS

Cost of drug patents to the NHS

Dear Sir,

The report by Nicholas Timmins (30 December) of Mr Justice Henry's ruling in favour of Smith, Kline and French against the DHSS on the matter of generic copies of drugs raises important questions for all those interested in the company's relationship between the NHS and the pharmaceutical industry.

The repeal of "licences of right" is contained in the Government's current Copyright, Designs and Patents Bill due shortly to finish its committee stage in the Lords. The industry undoubtedly has a case that it needs greater patent protection to cover development costs.

That is the rationale behind this clause in the Bill. But when it comes to be debated on 12 January, I shall be arguing strongly (and not alone) that there must be some corresponding safeguard for the development of the generics industry once a drug's patent has expired.

At a time of mounting alarm over NHS costs and their deferrment, anything that makes the production of generic copies "prohibitively expensive" is clearly against the national interest. It may not be possible to introduce an amendment into this Bill to ensure that generic copies may be produced for hospital use (and for prescription by GPs) but Dr Collier is surely right that the appropriate legislative vehicle will have to be found. I shall be pressing the Government on this point on 12 January and shall be interested to hear from anyone else who shares my concern. I exclude from this invitation lobbyists for the generics industry of whose views I am well aware!

Yours faithfully,
KIR MARNOCK
House of Lords
31 December

Trade union elections

Dear Sir,

Your labour editor's assertion (30 December) that "a list of sensible candidates has been circulated by officials of the right-wing electricians' union", in order to influence the outcome of the forthcoming elections for the Transport and General Workers' Union executive, would appear to be further evidence of the EEPTU encouraging privately what for many years it has publicly deplored — namely, outside interference in trade union elections.

The irony of David Felton's report can be best appreciated when it is realised that, in a union which holds elections for only a small executive (the rest of the officials are appointed and not accountable to the membership), the election procedure specifically forbids any circularisation (apart from the ballot paper) and indeed on occasions the EEPTU executive has used such "irregularities" to set aside elections!

Coming so soon after the furore surrounding the EEPTU's conduct at Wapping, with the resignation through 'ill health' of Tom Rice, the principal appointed official involved, and given the General Secretary's statement to the TUC that, 'the immediate responsibility for the actions of the union and that of its individual officers is mine . . .' the latest revelation can only add to the present disquiet surrounding the officers of the EEPTU.

Yours sincerely,
B. MUNRO
EEPTU member
(Southampton Branch)
London, N1
31 December

Road safety versus civil liberty

Dear Sir,

Some way of reducing road accidents would indeed involve an unacceptable encroachment on the liberties of mature and careful citizens in order to curb the activities of an irresponsible minority. But your leading article "Road safety versus civil liberty" (10 December) groups quite different possibilities together in a way that suggests there there is always a conflict between safety and liberty. Unless you believe that any rules restrict liberty, even the ordinary rules of the road such as driving on the left and stopping at traffic lights, that is not a tenable view.

The idea that a reduction in that national speed limit to, say 55mph, as in the USA, or 62mph as in New Zealand (both liberty-loving countries) would restrict freedom seems to depend on the view that most people can drive safely at high speeds even if a feckless few cannot. But speed increases risks for reasons connected with physical laws that apply to us all. Lower and better enforced speed limits would certainly reduce the number and severity of accidents; this was clearly established in our review of 30 schemes, drawn from a wide range of countries, published in 1984. They would also reduce the stress which many people now experience when driving on motorways and which deters others from using them altogether. Thus, freedom would be enhanced rather than reduced.

Unsafe conditions on other roads, arising from traffic moving too fast for their surroundings, encroach on fundamental liberties. In particular, parents have to deny their children the right to get about on their own, although that is essential to their healthy development. The time penalties that need to be imposed on motorists to make life safe for pedestrians and cyclists are trivial in comparison.

Yours faithfully,
Dr MAYER HILLMAN
STEPHEN PLOWDEN
Policy Studies Institute
London, NW1

Growing global body poetic

Dear Sir,

According to Elizabeth Jennings (31 December) "One only has to look at the poetry periodicals" to realise that "the once great exchange between the poetries of America and Great Britain has been almost completely ended". The last five issues of New Departures have presented no work by no less than 40 US poets alongside about twice as many of their British contemporaries — New Departures II, for example, included Corso, Creeley, Ginsberg, Guest, Calvin Hernton, Jack Hirschmann, Anselm Hollo, Lyn Lifshin, Loretta Schwartz and Jonathan Williams.

Miss Jennings may have been distracted by the overblown razmatazz of the "post-establishment" which, calling itself "post-modernist", "new narrative" or Martian, is indeed if anything even more resolute, Little England-ish and sometimes xenophobic than its parent generation. As the so-called Movement did: but neither of these incestuous groups genuinely did or could represent the essential energies of this country's body poetic, which is currently getting more and more audible and visible (especially by a younger public) as probably more global, as well as transatlantic, than at any previous point in time.

Yours superb faithfully,
MICHAEL HOROVITZ
Poetry Olympics
Stroud, Gloucestershire

Future facing the jobless

Dear Sir,

David Felton's piece in Thursday's Independent made quite clear for the first time the full extent of planned compulsion for Britain's unemployed. In future, long-term unemployed people will be compelled to participate in poor-quality training schemes followed by voluntary work with no financial reward for their efforts (except the continued payment of benefit plus pocket money to cover all or part of their work expenses) and probably no prospect of real work at the end of it.

In a full employment situation when unemployed people could find suitable work, compulsion has never proved necessary. With four million people unable to find permanent jobs and with only three quarters of a million vacancies, most of them in the very low paid and temporary or requiring skills not available amongst the unemployed, the victimisation of people already depressed, demoralised or even physically or mentally ill can only be described as immoral.

The meanmindedness of the latest policies is the more extreme when set in the context of the proposed £1bn budget handouts to people in work including those in the higher tax bracket.

The Chancellor knows that he could transform Britain's employment prospects by channelling £1bn gross (or £3bn net) into job creation and high quality training instead of tax cuts. He knows too, that aid more could be done if he were willing to do no more to cut the national debt than he did two years ago when a policy would require a dialogue with the trade unions and sensible policies to control inflation. Mass unemployment is a semaphore signature receiving, it seems, less political dangers.

Yours sincerely,
MOLLY MEACHER
Director
Campaign for Work
London N6
31 December

Mean awards

Dear Sir,

I write as a holder of the George Cross to express my unhappiness at the awards of the George Medal, one posthumous, to two people involved in the Herald of Free Enterprise disaster.

Incorporated in the warrant investigating the award for this recognition that the award winner's life must be seen to be at great risk. Surely both these men are worthy of the higher honour and I for one feel very aware that the episode which led to my George Cross pales by comparison with the occasion that merited the award of today's less prestigious George Medal.

Perhaps, with my tongue in my cheek, the fact that the George Cross includes an annual tax free award of £600 makes the present Government less willing to see Her Majesty award George Crosses.

In my humble opinion, both these men should have been awarded the George Cross.

Yours faithfully,
A. WALTON
Malvern, Worcestershire

Enjoying the chase

Dear Sir,

Your leader (28 December) "Suffering the hunt fraternity" reminded me of the several occasions I was taken cubbing at the age of 10, and came to watch a stag hunt in 1937.

The chase was exciting, with the huntsman's horn blowing and hounds racing after the fox whilst the field streamed across the countryside in pursuit. But the reality of the kill was quite horrible and, having been "blooded", I refused the "mask" covered in blood. For all that I was extremely angry. I had to accept two "pads" instead which were tied to my saddle and later mounted for display.

I can understand riders enjoying the chase but not why it has to be after a live animal. A "drag" is perfectly satisfactory and could easily be improved to include different sorts of trophy at the end and instead of a kill.

Yours sincerely,
D. BROTHERS
Oxford
29 December

Front-page data

Dear Sir,

May I suggest — as a New Year's resolution — that it would save a lot of people's time and trouble if everyone who issues documents of any sort were to ensure that the date of issue was clearly displayed on the front page or cover, preferably in the top right-hand corner, so that when documents are later consulted, or retrieved from files, their vintage is more clearly known. I am thinking of travel files, catalogues, price lists, reports, etc. If the source of your social also be displayed, that would be a bonus!

Yours truly,
DAVID SAWTELL
Stoke Roger, Buckinghamshire
2 December

Press embargoes

Dear Sir,

You were right to report on your front page (31 December) Mrs Thatcher's extreme annoyance at the breach, by The Sun newspaper, of the embargo on publications of names in the New Year Honours List.

I cannot speak for other trades unions in printing or journalism. But I can state categorically that such behaviour would not be tolerated in members of the Institute of Journalists whose code of professional ethics precludes such conduct. One sentence from the code says it all:

Moreover, examples, however induced, of acts that the highest standards of journalism reflect on the medium concerned and by bringing it into disrepute lessen the confidence of the public and raise the imposition of controls.

Heaven knows the public's esteem of journalists (as opposed to "freedom of the press") is low enough, as low as that of politicians (as opposed to "parliamentary democracy"). Your paper has highlighted, in the context of Mr Jeremy Warner being forced to reveal his sources of financial information under the 1981 Contempt of Court Act, how legislation can be introduced to narrow the freedom of the press.

My bet is that the present unpleasantness will harden Mrs Thatcher's attitude to the possible imposition of VAT on newspapers.

Yours very truly,
JOHN HART
General Secretary
Institute of Journalists
London, SE10

Phoney wars

Dear Sir,

I read with interest Peter Pringle's article "America prepares itself for the phoney war" (30 December) concerning the Pentagon's current case to build regiments of dummy tanks.

It reminded me of a conversation I had with a British veteran who had served in the desert campaign of the Second World War. He recounted to me the story of how the Allies had built an army of dummy tanks to mislead German intelligence. Unfortunately the ruse did not work out entirely as planned, for although the German bombers could not destroy the dummy tanks, they did so using wooden bombs!

Yours faithfully,
NICHOLAS PINK
Cambridge

'Living Arctic'

Dear Sir,

On 4 January an article by Rich and North on the native peoples of northern Canada (Saturday Magazine's current exhibition "Living Arctic" is partly funded by the Institute of Canada.

I would like to point out that in fact the British Museum, of which the Museum of Mankind is the Ethnography Department, has accepted no sponsorship from the fur trade.

Yours respectfully,
ANDREW HAMILTON
British Museum
London, WC1

Lasting lessons from the class of '68

By Peter Jenkins

REMEMBRANCES of the year 1968 have begun. A flood of books* and films are on the way. Yet in Britain (although not in Northern Ireland) 1968 was a largely non-eventful year. There were some student protests but it was mild stuff compared with what had been going on in Berkeley, Berlin and the Italian universities. We seemed, as ever, mainly interested in the protests in our pockets and in our pay packets: it was the year after devaluation, the year before the débacle of In Place of Strife, the Wilson government's attempt to reform our thoroughly industrial relations.

Nevertheless, the events and ideas of that year shook the world by its post-war foundations. In France the students very nearly did bring down Général de Gaulle no less. In America the anti-war movement effectively ended the presidency of Lyndon Johnson. The militants of French workers who joined in what was for the most part a spontaneous general strike had to be bought off with a whopping 14 per cent pay increase. The events of 1968 gave a powerful twist to the great inflation which was to have so profound an effect on the 1970s. De Gaulle correctly saw 1968 as a "revolt against consumer society, against technological society, whether communist in the East or capitalist in the West." It was also the climax of a generation conflict and an explosion of moral indignation, against the war in Vietnam in particular and the oppression and exploitation of the Third World in general.

Like a real revolution, the French "revolution" of 1968 passed through classic stages. Its original leaders were co-opted by fantasies of direct democracy. Instrumental goals gave way to transformational dreams. For the politics of 1968 had deep existential roots. The revolutionary students read the equivalent of their 16 Brumaire at the Renault plant at Billancourt on 17 May, when the Communist-led unions looked the

main gates against their Stalinist ally out on the side of reaction in France no less than in Czechoslovakia.

Although 1968 proved to be in Britain its main legacies washed against our shores. Against a background of political activism and ideological enthusiasm Wilsonian "democratic" came to seem a plodding, shoddy project. In Britain the Labour Movement became the short victim of Rab Dahrendorf's "long march through the institutions."

Edward Heath succeeded Wilson but his inheritance was a country increasingly unwilling to be governed. To be governed? To be too much less unforgiving life is to get rid of the politicians," said Dany Cohn-Bendit. The disastrous and discplinous of representative democracies had then undermined by new notions of participatory democracy. New styles of industrial militancy were in vogue. The new wind radical was practised by the workers who occupied Upper Clyde Shipbuilders and by Ar that straight in the Yorkshire coalfield, culminated by the downfall of the Heath government. In this way he had become most of it to keep the spirit of 68.

The "class of '68" — which is a shorthand for the graduates of the period that 1967 graduates of the school sense and of the university of political culture — played a major part in the shaping of British politics during the subsequent years. That mostly a black and roadside student became a new generation now a generation of our own politics became a new phenomenon in the picking-up of the political and our general now 1968 ideas Keir Livingstone and the "loony left" are among its children.

But even then these radicals, equally inimical to establishment and freedom consumer society were essentially concerned with their own individual experience and experience. Their first popularism was an old against the authority of the English against compromise and establishment. It was also against an old disposition to deny power to its own purpose. Thatcherism perhaps an idiom of the English against compromise and estab-

a victim of the spirit of 68.

The "class of '68"

* For examples, Ronald Fraser, 1968 to be published by Chatto and Windus, and David Caute, Sixty-eight: Year of the Barricades, by Hamish Hamilton, both in January.

The beggar's opera house

As Covent Garden stretches out its hand for more, Robert Maycock looks at opera funding abroad

One of the traditional national rituals of the year's end is a short trot between two voices with chorus starring the Royal Opera House and the Arts Council. The scene is a wintry landscape in which the Government has not persuaded enough money to go round for the following year. Shortly before the Arts Council meets to divide the money among the deserving poor, the house issues an annual report and passionately deplores the meagreness of its portion. The council ponders weightily and replies in tones of deep regret with an increase that does not meet the house's needs. From the chorus comes the refrain: "They do these things so much better abroad". But do they? It depends

where you look. This year the annual report has itself taken the unusual step of comparing the Royal Opera House's finances for the 1987/88 season with those of six houses on the Continent. In terms of total budget, the Royal Opera House falls in the middle of the range, though with three companies to run — the Royal Opera, the Royal Ballet and Sadler's Wells Royal Ballet — it gives more performances than any of the others. The notable differences begin when the sources of income are analysed.

Five of the houses, including Paris, Vienna and three in West Germany, receive 72 to 73 per cent of their income in the form of grants. The sixth, Berlin, receives 81 per cent. For the Royal Opera House, the figure is only 46 per cent. Covent Garden finds 42 per cent of, its income as "house receipts", while the others only have to earn 17 to 27 per cent. Sponsorship in London is eight times higher than the nearest figures elsewhere, and it is the only house to show a projected deficit. The message is clear: British public funding does not bear comparison with that of Europe's. The season's new chairman, Sir John Sainsbury, in his first foreword, writes of "a serious under-funding of our activities" and adds another set of figures showing that over the past five years the house's grant has declined in four years from 54 per cent.

The basis of the comparisons is open to some criticism. The houses differ in the scale of their operation, the number of theatres they use and the number of companies they run; and the figures do not come from published

sources. Philip Jones, the Royal Opera House's director of finance, says that they were requested in a letter form Sir John Tooley, the general director, to his opposite numbers, and that the questions were clearly put. All the companies' in-house performances and external activities were to be included, irrespective of the number of venues.

The head of the Arts Council's information unit, Rod Fisher, is about to conduct a more detailed survey of the European opera scene. While he does not yet have recent figures to set against the Royal Opera, he believes that "the ROH is right in percentage terms. In Europe, the box-office contribution is usually 10 to 30 per cent. In British houses, it is usually between 30 and 60 per cent."

As it happens, the Royal Opera House does not quote the most spectacular examples of subsidy: the Nordic opera houses. Two years ago, the Norwegian Opera had to raise only 13 to 14 per cent of its budget by its own activities and received the rest from government. Less surprisingly, the Metropolitan Opera House in New York is unrated. The position here radically changes the context of the Royal Opera

House report. According to figures obtained from the Met for 1986/85, the latest year available, nearly 60 per cent of the house's revenue was earned: 51.3 per cent from the box office and 8.4 per cent from visiting companies, the broad heading of "contributions" amounts to 33.3 per cent. Profits less than a third of this figure comes from public funds. The Met would not give details of donations, but it is well known that in the USA, individual giving

Past disasters, future unease: Covent Garden is under threat from more energetic fund-raisers

> British public funding does not bear comparison with the rest of Europe

> It would be naïve to think the US model could be imposed on Covent Garden

fic Americans on the other hand, would look upon it as positively feather-bedded.

On the face of it, these differences do not appear crucial to what goes on stage; both the Royal Opera House and the Met are still among the great international houses, even if the Royal Opera House's position seems precarious. It would be naive for hawkish people to think that the American model could be imposed on Covent Garden. What the differences represent is deeply rooted within the various national cultures. The Nordic model of social responsibility with strong ethical-moral overtones has its adherents in British arts circles, but has never penetrated the political Establishment here. And the level of private giving taken for granted in America could only be built on over decades, even if there were better tax incentives.

For the same reason, an "emergency" government grant to the biggest company would look monstrously wrong. Yet sponsorship is also not a panacea as has remained at 8 per cent of Royal Opera House income for several years. Video and media exploitation has picked design paltering returns. The house's move into property development is meant to pay for the rest of the work on a final redevelopment that also not to run the show. Without a certain expansion that means great support, the arts still be pressed back to individuals, who will either bake to pay more freely than for lack of choice (for lack cheaper productions or fewer houses). Because is able to compete in an international market more need to divert public money and raise extra support that could

> Increasing funds would be at the expense of other Arts Council clients

the level it was three years ago in real terms, would require an increase of more than 11 per cent on what we will receive this year." But any increase would be at the expense of other Arts Council clients, and would be especially partly to the regional opera companies.

These companies are already caught within a poverty trap which makes them lose money for every performance they give. They cannot raise much more at the box office than they already do for fear of losing the audiences they have painfully developed. With inadequate subsidy they are driven into cheaper productions or fewer performances. Because it is able to compete in an international market more readily than its regional rivals for public and private money, the big house would be likely to gain most. It would not only win the funding battle but in the process lay the audiences.

The advantages in being camera shy

Julian Critchley on the expedience of televising the Commons

DO MPs behave badly and, if so, should the television cameras be kept from the Chamber until we mend our ways? "Sources close to Downing Street" have let it be known that Mrs Thatcher will not be in favour of the cameras in the Commons when the matter is debated early this year. In the past she has appeared irresolute, believing in the broadcasting of the House of Commons in principle but against it in practice. For this reason her proxies in the Cabinet — the big battalions — may well vote against. A three-line Whip would turn the trick.

Should it be? Isn't that what Parliament is for?

The House of Commons, its members draws up facing one another as if on the field of Waterloo, serves as a substitute for violence. Before a raspberry blown at the Government front bench it is beaten; a punch thrown at Nigel Lawson. Parliament is not the House of the Church of England, the purpose of its existence is a Council of state: it is an arena specifically designed for confrontational politics and it all becomes those who have deliberately sharpened the divisions between Government and Opposition — for example, that the Conservatives can be by two by the "old consensus" to behave like moderate assess in a public bar. I think it was Enoch Powell who said that humbug is the essential courtesy of public life: if so, the most have had this restraint to mind.

It is humbug to serve up a sequestered disapproval of a rowdy Commons as the reason for voting against the televising of the House. One might as well argue that exposure to a shocked and disapproving public would oblige the more adventurous to amend their ways. But that is not the point. It is extraordinary that the public is denied a glimpse of the Commons while being fed a diet of more decorous debate from the House of Lords. And to be denied it on the grounds of purely disadvantage.

Let me explain. What are the reasons put forward to those who would prevent the cameras from entering? Strip aside the rationalisations and the special pleading — for example, that the Commons would be distorted by the television set of the news media — and we are left with the effect of television on the standing of Government and party. The fear too much would be shown to the by-and-

been discouraged by the pro-leagues and by the lack of attention on the part of the press to anything that happens after five o'clock in the afternoon.

Mrs Thatcher, John Wakeham, David Waddington and Peter Brooke, Chairman of the Conservative Party, must take into account the political effect of television upon the Government's fortunes. John Biffen would have been its acceptable face, but he is an exile. Michael Heseltine are perforce better than our modest of the Cabinet, none of whom, save Douglas Hurd and Peter Walker, can make a decent speech. Most of the junior ministers have difficulty reading their scripts, some even sound convinced over the loss of a wireless with words, sadly to shine quite in most and swapping televised sincerities to the fallen end.

If Mrs Thatcher votes against the cameras it will not be because she is fearful of the effect of the party backbenchers' behaviour on the public mind. She will do it because she is a conventional Prime Minister's Questions how would those two periods of 15 minutes go down?

I think rather badly. She could win a sympathetic one-woman confrontation on more ground over four minutes for 15 minutes by and she has not shown much real grasp of the Opposition as she should; it is the place of which she has shown her genuine lust for power. How might those two periods of 15 minutes go down?

---

*The Jenkins book welcomes letters...

During the first year this consolidation has extended across the newspaper. There is a view that having established our upmarket position it must be held and expanded. In design terms, this is perceived as a reluctance to use logos or typography which in any way smacks of tabloid or downmarket newspapers. Artistically too, this view has wide currency. At the start when everyone was rushing around chasing their own and other people's tails, it was easy to fall into the trap of allowing too many logos to be commissioned through the design department for a variety of editorial columns from Armchair Investor on the City pages to Alan Watkins on Rugby on the Sports pages. Having designed many of these, it was difficult to control them, such was the internal structure of the nightly production cycle and the practice of departmental responsibility. Most of the illustrated logos have now been dropped. A greater reliance on typographical logos has been adopted; this works extremely well with the generally clean appearance of the newspaper. The exception remains the Weekend section and the Sports Department where a more exciting, sporting image is maintained.

Although from the start, white on black headings or WOBs had been banned, the advocates of BOTs or black on tints had managed to fight a rearguard action. The News In Brief columns began their life in this form but BOTs have now been dropped apart from in the advertising columns, the listings pages and on shares prices.

During the past year, the Fashion page has become less adventurous and fussy and more refined. Earlier in *The Independent* it was used almost experimentally to test the range of the computer layout system and the capability of the production processes.

For some months up to the first anniversary, 7 October 1987, I and others had been unhappy with the excess of logos and typographical differences on the Business and City pages. One problem lay in the necessarily large volume of short stories carried in those departments and the number of daily statistical tables that were necessary. Ruby Gordon, a staff designer, and I redesigned the furniture or regular standing items and the new look, complete with a redesigned thinner version of the Oxford rule began to appear in the week starting 7 December 1987. I say began to appear because of the time taken to format new design into the computer system for regular use. For example, one fairly simple looking logo made up by hand can take several hours to reproduce and then program with all the possible variables into the layout data base. Once there the speed of use is invaluable.

A remarkable feature of the first year was the number of awards and prizes won by *The Independent*. Each week's postbag seemed to bring in yet another accolade. From Newspaper of the Year, to Journalist of the Year (AWS) to Medium of the Year, they flowed in. To the design department, the prize most coveted was winning that of best designed newspaper in the national newspaper category of the Newspaper Design Awards.

In his speech at the presentation ceremony at the House of Commons on 2 September, AWS summed up the problems over designing a newspaper: 'Of all the requirements of bringing a new newspaper to the market, much the hardest work has been design. It was the subject which gave us the most serious pre-launch headaches because there are no certainties in design.

'I found that there is scarcely a journalist who isn't an expert on design. Those of my colleagues who would scarcely express an opinion on money supply, apart from financial journalists, or on the future of David Owen, apart from political journalists, all had an opinion on design.'

He said that using on-screen layout at *The Independent* had given back to the editorial team full responsibility for the creative input of the paper.

In their report, the NDA judges said: 'Instinctively we all liked *The Independent*. It was our idea of what that sort of newspaper should look like; a real newspaper, reassuring, authoritative. Its picture treatments are marvellous, so much so that someone actually criticised them for being too good in looking more like works of art than newspaper pix.'

By August 1987 everyone knew that editorial spending at *The Independent* was higher than had been anticipated in the prospectus, mainly because of increases in staff, especially in the production and classified advertising departments. A ban on the recruitment of staff was implemented and departmental heads were warned to keep strictly within their budgets. AWS remained convinced that it would be wrong to go back to the shareholders for more money. He was determined that the newspaper would break even.

'The motto I'd like everyone to have above their desk is: "No Profits, No Independence". If we want to retain control over our destiny, we've got to bite the bullet and keep a tight control of costs and keep the lid on them,' he said in September. As the year ended the newspaper was turning the corner and heading for a confirmed profit.

The advertising volumes for Fleet Street for a week taken at random from 14 September to 19 September 1987 showed how well *The Independent* was doing: out of a total pagination of 192, the paper had 15 classified advertising pages and 46 display advertising pages; *The Times*' figures respectively were 260, 45 and 50; *The Guardian*, 204, 47 and 30.

In the same month readership profiles of the quality dailies from November 1986 to June 1987 were published. *The Independent* came second to the *Financial Times* as the most male-biased title, in percentages 71.1 readers of the FT were men and 68 for *The Independent* (*The Times* 62.7, *The Daily Telegraph* 53.8, *The Guardian* 60.4). But in the 'yuppie' category, the figures showed the strength of *The Independent* which had 48.5 per cent of its readers in the 15–34 range (*The Times* 36.7, *The Daily Telegraph* 25, *The Guardian* 43.80, the *FT* 41.6). In social terms the figures were as follows, ABC1 *The Independent* 80.3 (*The Times* 83.5, *The Daily Telegraph* 81.0, *The Guardian* 80.2, the *FT* 83.4). The pattern and consolidation was continuing apace. In the National Readership Survey research for April to September 1987, 82 per cent of the readers were in the ABC1 category and 71 per cent were under 45. By November between 53–55 per cent of copies read were through home deliveries.

In retrospect *The Independent* has proved an exciting and well-conceived success. Judgement allied to a lot of luck and the commitment of all those working for the newspaper has helped to ensure and consolidate that success. The combination of business acumen and journalistic excellence has proved, or will shortly do so, that it is possible to launch a newspaper and turn the enterprise into a profit-making concern within 18 months. The advantages of web-offset printing are inescapable. The clarity and appeal of the photographs is at once a product of good photography and of high-resolution printing. Another important advantage of web-offset printing is that less ink comes off on one's hands.

Timing was everything. Had the Wapping dispute not occurred, perhaps far fewer journalists would have left *The Times* and *The Sunday Times*; equally, perhaps fewer readers would have switched to *The Independent*. The Stock Market crash of late autumn 1987 would have made it much more difficult to raise the money had it occurred earlier.

Technology has played a major part in that success. The speed of typesetting by journalists and the ease of making up pages is an integral part of its achievements. The cleanness of the layout stems directly from the computer precision of on-screen make-up. No human eye or hand could hope to provide the consistency of spacing and rule work between headlines and stories.

Yards away from *The Independent* building Defoe is happily turning in his grave. It is characteristic of this great Nonconformist that in his *Essay On Literature*, he was mainly concerned with technology, with the making of books rather than the writing of them. He illustrates how the development of printing led to 'the spreading of useful Knowledge in the World, making the Accession of it cheap and easy'. Perhaps he was predicting how *The Independent* would flourish 260 years later.

Glossary

Blackletter: form of bold lettering for title-pieces, now old-fashioned.

Black or bold: Bold-faced text or headline type.

Body type: the type used in articles, as opposed to headlines.

By-line: Name of writer or photographer.

Column rule: A light rule used to separate columns in a newspaper.

Deck: Section of headline, not line; a three-deck headline could have as many as eight lines.

Digitise: Copy material into the form of numbers for later reproduction as visible or legible matter.

Dummy: Sample page

Em: The square of the body of any size of type; usually meant as 12pt or pica em.

Facsimile transmission: Sending material, documents or entire newspages down a telephone line to a receiver in another location.

File: Entry made into the computer as an article, story, copy, headline or page layout by a journalist.

Filename: Name attached to a particular file for recall or recognition (Replaces traditional noun, catchline).

Font: Complete range of characters of any typeface or size.

Format: computer instructions to run software.

GT68: Name of VDT used for on-screen layout.

Hyphenate and justify: Automatic equalisation of space in each line of text to fill the line and break, or hyphenate, words according to a built-in memory.

Lead (pronounced 'led'): Strips of metal used to space out headlines and text; space between headlines or text.

Linotype: An old-fashioned type-composing machine.

Livery: folio, running head etc., or the type at the top of the page.

Masthead: A newspaper's main title line.

Measure: Width to which type is set.

Pica: The old name for 12pt. The pica em is the standard measure of width: a 10-em column is 10 pica ems in width.

Point: The basic unit of measuring type, despite metrication; there are 72 pts to the inch; point sizes range from $4\frac{3}{4}$pt to 300pts or so on some tabloid newspapers.

Sans serif, or sans: 'Modern' typefaces without curly 'serifs'.

Scan: to reproduce an image in digital form for printing.

Screen: Display front of VDT; number of dots per square inch on a half-tone picture.

Scroll: to view text by running from top to bottom on a computer screen.

Text: The reading type in a newspaper, as opposed to headlines.

Further Reading:

Allen Hutt, *The Changing Newspaper* (Gordon Fraser, London, 1973)

Allen Hutt, *Newspaper Design* (Oxford University Press, London, 1967)

Harold Evans, *Editing and Design, Book Five — Newspaper Design* (Heinemann, London, 1976; second edition)

'Raising venture capital for *The Independent*',(Venture Capital Report Ltd., Henley-on-Thames)

Iverach McDonald, *The History of The Times, Volume V 1939 – 1966* (Times Books, London, 1984)

Leslie Sellers, *Doing It In Style* (Pergamon Press, 1968)

Daniel Defoe, edited by James T. Boulton (Batsford, London 1965)

Index